Pizarro and the Conquest of Peru

By Frederick Ober

Introduction

This is a biography of one of Spain's most notorious explorers and conquistadores, Francisco Pizarro. Naturally, as one of the best known conquistadors, Francisco Pizarro (1471/6-1541) is also one of the most controversial. Like Christopher Columbus and Hernan Cortés before him, Pizarro was celebrated in Europe for subduing the Inca Empire, a culture that fascinated his contemporaries. At the same time, naturally, indigenous views of the man have been overwhelmingly negative. .

If Columbus and Cortés were the pioneers of Spain's new global empire, Pizarro consolidated its immense power and riches, and his successes inspired a further generation to expand Spain's dominions to unheard of dimensions. Furthermore, he participated in the forging of a new culture: like Cortés, he took an indigenous mistress with whom he had two mixed-race children, and yet the woman has none of the lasting fame of Cortés's Doña Marina. With all of this in mind, it is again remarkable that Pizarro remains one of the less well-known and less written about of the explorers of his age.

On the other hand, there are certain factors that may account for the conqueror of Peru's relative lack of lasting glory. For one, he was a latecomer in more than one sense. Cortés's reputation was built on being the first to overthrow a great empire, so Pizarro's similar feat, even if it bore even greater fruit in the long run, would always be overshadowed by his predecessor's precedent. But Pizarro also lacked the youthful glamour of Cortés: already a wizened veteran in his 50s by the time he undertook his momentous expedition, he proceeded with the gritty determination of a hardened soldier rather than the audacity and cunning of a young courtier.

AUTHORITIES

ON
FRANCISCO PIZARRO
XVITH CENTURY. Herrera, Antonio de (1552-1625), and Oviedo y Valdes (1478-1557) cover completely doings in the "Indies," including the conquest of Peru. The latter, Oviedo, was personally acquainted with Pizarro, as he accompanied Pedrarias to Darien in 1514, and was at Panama when the expedition was fitted out at that point for Peru.
Pedro Pizarro's *Relaciones del Descubrimiento y Conquista de los Reynos del Peru*, though finished by 1571, was not published until two hundred and fifty years later.
XVIITH CENTURY. The same may be said of Fernando Pizarro y Orellana, who wrote and published (Madrid, 1639) the *Varones Ilústres del Nuevo Mundo*, which contains lives of the Pizarros and Almagro.
Garcilasso de la Vega (the "Inca Garcilasso") (1539-1616) published a monumental work on Peru (Lisbon, 1609; Cordova, 1617), for the writing of which he was peculiarly fitted by birth and education. Though largely quoted by those who came after him, he is not held to be always accurate.
XVIIITH CENTURY. The story of Peru is well told in Robertson's *America*; but "by far the best life of Pizarro" is contained in the *Vidas de Espanoles Célebres*, by Don Manuel Josef Quintana (Madrid, 1807); *Pizarro and Balboa*, in English, 1832.
XIXTH CENTURY. The XlXth century also witnessed the forthcoming of such great works as Help's, Prescott's, and Markham's. Help's *Life of Pizarro* consists of material from his Spanish Conquest, and conspicuously exhibits the peculiarities of its author.
Of Prescott's *Conquest of Peru*, which was first published in 1843, and soon translated into all the languages of Europe, it seems almost superfluous to remark that it is by far the most comprehensive "popular" treatment of the subject, and at the same time exhaustive and critical. The narrative of the conquest, of which Pizarro was the central figure, cannot be dissociated from its hero, who is vividly portrayed by the great historian.

PIZARRO

PIZARRO

I

IN THE LAND OP POISONED ARROWS

1510-1519

FOUR hundred years ago the continent of South America was known to the world at large only as a vast wilderness inhabited by savages. But a few points had been touched at here and there on its northeastern coast, and no expeditions of discovery had been made to its unknown interior. Columbus, Vespucius, Pinzon, and others had sailed along certain sections of the coast, but behind the barrier of its mountains all was mystery. It was called, indeed, and for many years after the first landing of Spaniards in the West Indies remained, the "mysterious continent."
It is on the northern coast of this continent, in the year 1510, that we obtain our first glimpse of Francisco Pizarro. He had sailed thither from Santo Domingo, in an expedition commanded by

Alonzo de Ojeda, a cavalier renowned for his lion-like courage, but whose impetuous bravery always led him into disaster. His lieutenant, Pizarro, was equally brave and resolute, but cool and calculating, even in the midst of perils; and thus we see him the first time he looms upon the horizon of history, sturdily defending himself against the attacks of desperate Indian hordes. Behind him and his companions lay the interminable forest, which, swarming with hostile Indians, enveloped them on every side save in front, where stretched the sea, but upon which they could not embark unless some were left to perish. His commander had been given the governorship of a province on the isthmus of Darien; but he had to conquer that province first, and as it was occupied by natives who fancied they had a better right to it than Ojeda – as they really had – and as they were, moreover, fierce and warlike, being allied to the cannibal Caribs of the islands, he found himself engaged in war at the outset.

There were no braver men in the world than the Spaniards of those days, seasoned by their wars with the Moors and their many encounters with the American Indians, and, as every foe they met had been overcome, they held these natives of the New World in contempt, from the ease with which they were vanquished. There was hardly a Spaniard who did not consider himself a match for at least a score of Indians, clad as he was in his impenetrable armor of steel, and armed with keen-edged sword or arquebuse; while his naked enemy was almost defenceless, his rude weapons consisting solely of war-club and javelin, or lance of fire-hardened wood, with bow and arrows. But these natives of "Terra Firma" – as the north coast was called – possessed a weapon which made them for a time the equals of the Spaniards. It was the terrible poisoned arrow, dipped in the deadly *curari*, or *woorari*, prepared by them in the secret recesses of the forests. Clouds of these envenomed arrows assailed the Spaniards as they landed on the hostile shore; but they did not heed them, having hitherto considered an arrow-wound as of no consequence. When, however, soldier after soldier dropped to the ground in most excruciating torments, which were swiftly ended by inevitable death, the survivors became panic-stricken. Ojeda thus lost seventy of his men in his first encounter with the Indians of Terra Firma, and was himself wounded in the thigh, and would certainly have died but for his heroic remedy, which he made his surgeon apply, on pain of death for refusal. Wrenching the envenomed arrow from the wound, he enclosed his thigh between two red-hot plates of iron. By this means the poison was expelled, though the limb was scorched and shrivelled; but he survived, while his pilot, the gallant Juan de la Cosa, died from a similar wound, after his body had swollen to twice its natural size.

Although equally exposed with Ojeda, Francisco Pizarro survived this skirmish with the Indians unharmed, to make his bow to posterity. He was simply a soldier of fortune, seeking adventure as another man might have sought game in the forest or fish in the sea. He had enlisted as a private in the expedition; but when at last it became necessary for Ojeda to return to Santo Domingo for reinforcements, he was left in command of the decimated company, and in this capacity showed his abilities.

It is doubtful if he ever before aspired to leadership, being apparently contented with his position in the ranks; but he accepted what was thrust upon him without protest, and did his duty as before. He promised Ojeda to await his return during fifty days; but thenceforth ill-luck pursued the gallant leader to the verge of the grave, which he found in Santo Domingo at the end of this very voyage. He never returned to succor his companions, and in this manner, as the leader of a forlorn hope against starvation and violence, Pizarro found his first command.

Never was an inexperienced commander left in a more perilous situation. Turn whichever way he would, he found himself menaced by a danger. Inland stretched the vast forest, which white men had scarcely penetrated but which was alive with hostile savages. The bay upon which the projected settlement had been begun opened invitingly to the sea, upon which was safety, and beyond were friends. But the two small vessels left by Ojeda could not carry the company, and there was no alternative but to wait until famine, assisted by the Indians with their poisoned arrows, had sufficiently thinned out that devoted band. It was a dreadful choice – of death by starvation or by violence – but Pizarro grimly accepted the hard conditions, and, intrenching himself behind palisades of palm-logs, awaited the inevitable ending. It came in about six months, when there remained only men enough to fill the brigantines. They killed the horses they had saved for this emergency, salted their meat for sea-stores, and embarked.

While as a hero of history Francisco Pizarro cannot be ignored, it may be truthfully urged that he was not an ideal one. As we proceed in the history of his life we shall discover that though he remains to the end patient, persevering, and uncomplaining – possesses, in fact, many admirable qualities – he is ever brutal, cold-blooded in his cruelties, calculating in his villanies. While he remains in the ranks, and even when holding a little brief authority, his baser qualities do not appear; but it is probably because he has not become so prominent as to command attention.

And yet, perhaps, an excuse may be found, not only in the circumstances of his early life, but in those by which he was surrounded when first we find him. His heart may have been seared by the horrors of that long wait in the wilderness, when he was compelled, day after day, to witness the death-throes of comrades; to repel attacks by the savages; to steel himself against the cries of the wounded and dying; to hold himself, through it all, ready for any emergency. He was coarse by nature, perhaps brutal; but the sufferings of that six months' siege probably made him callous, and insensible to sympathy. Upon some natures this terrible experience would have operated towards the softening of their hearts; but Francisco Pizarro seems to have been made of that stern stuff which hardens in the fire of affliction.

It was his intention to sail direct for Santo Domingo, whence he had come; but when only a few leagues from shore he was met by an expedition under command of one Enciso, a lawyer, with reinforcements and provisions. As soon as Enciso, who had come out as Ojeda's partner, learned that the famished men were deserting their post, he was for putting them all in irons; but he was resisted by Pizarro, who compelled him to furnish them with supplies, which he did on condition that they would return to the settlement.

It seemed fated that Pizarro should not leave the isthmus until he had discovered certain things which led up, step by step, to the conquest he achieved a few years later. His better judgment urged him to return to Santo Domingo, but by the arrival of Enciso he was now only second in command, and compelled to obey him. He submitted without a murmur, for, in whatever school he had been trained, previous to his ventures in America, he had learned to obey.

The three vessels sought the harbor of San Sebastian – as the settlement had been named – but it was with reluctance that those who had suffered there so acutely returned, and the very fact that Enciso forced them to do so excited a dissension which resulted in his ruin. They found the palisades broken down, and the Indians, who had destroyed it, as expert as ever in the use of poisoned arrows. They caused such consternation that, though one of the vessels had foundered, carrying down nearly all their provisions, they resolved to evacuate San Sebastian and seek another refuge.

They were reduced to the verge of starvation; but after subsisting awhile upon the buds of palm-trees and the flesh of such animals as they could find in the forest, they were saved by a man who had not been invited to become one of their number, but who had come out from Santo Domingo headed-up in a barrel. This man was Vasco Nuñez de Balboa, who, of course, is known to every reader of history as the discoverer of the Pacific. When he had broken out of his barrel and made his appearance before Enciso on shipboard in mid-sea, that worthy was for throwing him overboard at once; for as a lawyer he knew the risks in protecting a man who, like Balboa, had run away from his creditors. It would have been better for Enciso had he carried out his original intention, for Balboa was largely responsible for his downfall when, elected *alcalde* of the second settlement these wanderers founded, he expelled the lawyer from their midst.

For the time, however, Balboa was the savior of the starving colonists, as he led them to an Indian village, far inland, where they found not only provisions in abundance, but golden idols, chains, and breast-plates in the greatest profusion. These inland Indians, unfortunately for them, did not use the poisoned arrow, so the Spaniards, weak and famishing as they were, had everything their own way. They slashed the poor natives with their swords, pierced them with lances, shot them down with arquebuses, and, after making many prisoners, founded near the site of their village the. town of Antigua.

At this point the fortunes of Balboa and Pizarro rise, in proportion as those of Enciso descend. With the expulsion of the unfortunate lawyer from the colony, we have nothing to do, for it is the fortune of the patient, plodding, and as yet unambitious Pizarro that we are following. Many years later Enciso cast Pizarro into prison on account of his share in the proceedings against him at Antigua; but that will be mentioned when we come to it. For a brief period of his career Pizarro 's fate and Balboa's became, as it were, intertwined, for they were much alike and the best of comrades; but so long as they were together, the "man-of-the-barrel" was ever the leader, and the common soldier seemed content to have it so.

While he held a subordinate position, it appears, Pizarro never quarrelled with his companions, either of his own rank or with those above him. He was a model soldier, and in many respects an admirable man – of a sort, but not the sort that would command admiration or respect at the present day. . . .

Pizarro was always at the beck and call of Balboa, and if he ever protested against the treatment of Ojeda's partner, and that of the still more unfortunate Nicuesa (who was not only deprived of his province, but set adrift to perish in obscurity), no record has been made of the fact. He became captain of a company, and that seemed to be the limit of his ambition. But he was a good captain, good to his men, faithful to his commander, hesitating at no difficult duty assigned him, balking at no peril or prospective danger.

Sent out by Balboa in search of gold, he discovered a province in which the sepulchres of the natives were full of treasure in the shape of little golden gods and ornaments. Despatched against the hostile Indians of the mountains far from the coast, he defeated them with great slaughter, though having with him a mere handful of fighting-men. For they lacked that weapon of which mention has been made – the poisoned arrow.

It is strange that, while the mountaineers made no use of this effective arm against the invaders of their territory, the natives of the coast, from Paria to Darien, all possessed it. An Italian who visited the north coast of South America about the middle of the sixteenth century wrote: "The principal arms the Indians carry are bows with poisoned arrows, which they make either of palm wood or of slender river reeds; and instead of iron at the point they tie hard fish-scales or pieces of flint, anointing them with a black bitumen which is a pure venom, made from roots, herbs, ants, and some other beastly mixtures, and then moistened with snake's blood, by old women, who boil it with great diligence until it is brought to perfection; and owing to the injurious vapors which rise from it, most of these women die in consequence. When the fluid is fresh, the man's body that is wounded with it swells inwardly and he soon dies mad. But if the poison has been prepared a long time it loses a great part of its strength and deadly virus, so that the wounded man may be cured by a red-hot iron, with which his wound is seared, and thus he does not die." The same traveller states that after Enciso had been expelled from Darien, Balboa started inland in search of gold. He made friends with some Indian chiefs, one of whom was called Panciaco, and was baptized by the Spaniards as Don Carlos. "He gave them a certain quantity of gold; but seeing how they quarrelled in the sharing of it, with one hand he tossed it all out of the scales onto the ground, saying: 'I am not a little surprised that you Christians make such a fuss about so vile a thing, as if it were good to eat or to drink! But since you have so great a desire for this metal, I will lead you to a place where you all may satisfy yourselves with it.' He then conducted them to the great Southern Ocean. Balboa, on account of the great riches that he found in this province, named it the Golden Castile, and there the city of Panama is now established."

On another expedition, led by Pizarro, a *cacique* named Careta was captured, whose daughter, said to be a comely maiden, Balboa took as his wife, thus making an ally of an Indian who might have proved a determined enemy. Through this maiden, or her father, Balboa first heard of the great Southern Ocean, which we now know as the Pacific, and, being seconded by his indomitable captain, Francisco Pizarro, he determined to seek it out. The journey was long, and for a great part of the distance lay through the hostile territory of King Ponca, who was finally converted from foe to friend, and consented to guide them to the ocean.

After more than three weeks in the forests, enduring terrible privations, the summit of a lofty mountain appeared above the wilderness of trees. Before they reached it, however, they were assailed by the hostiles of another tribe, of whom the Spaniards killed more than six hundred, from their deserted huts securing vast treasure in pearls and gold. They found, also, what was then to them of more importance, an abundant supply of food. Encouraged by the evidence of wealth in this new country, and refreshed by their repasts, after so much suffering, Balboa and Pizarro pressed forward with renewed energy, accompanied by less than fourscore men of their command, the others having fallen out by the way. Still with them, however, was the famous bloodhound, Leoncito, who had torn so many Indians in pieces that he was a host in himself, and at sight of whom the timid natives fled in affright.

At last, right in front of them rose the craggy peak which King Ponca had pointed out at a distance and from which, he said, the great Southern Ocean might be seen. Commanding his men to wait till further orders, Balboa climbed eagerly to the summit, desirous to be the first to view that watery world which had thus far eluded the search of all explorers, including Columbus, the first, and himself, the last.

Its magnitude, its extent, he may not have imagined; but whatever it might be, he, Balboa, was the first white man to gaze upon it, and, if the records may be credited, Captain Pizarro was the second. For, after sinking upon his knees and offering thanks to God for the great favor which had been granted him, Balboa rose and waved his hands to his companions as a signal to join him. Led by their captain, they pressed forward rapidly, scrambling to the peak beside him, whence they gazed enraptured upon the shimmering surface of the ocean, like a silver crescent in the distance, with vast stretch of intervening forests beautiful to behold.

This notable event occurred on September 25, 1513, at which date Francisco Pizarro had passed more than three years in the vast forest-wilderness of Darien.

II

WITH BALBOA IN DARIEN

1513-1517

AT the time he was permitted by Providence to behold that glorious panorama of sea and land, unfolded from the isolated peak in Darien, Francisco Pizarro was more than forty years of age, having been born in or about the year 1471. His birthplace was Truxillo, Spain, in the province of Estremadura, from which also hailed Hernando Cortés, who, though fifteen years his junior, was to achieve the conquest of Mexico before Pizarro had even heard of Peru. The two were related, through the mother of Cortés and the father of Pizarro; but they did not meet in their youth, owing to the fact that the latter, though acknowledging the paternity of Francisco, was never married to his mother. The elder Pizarro, Gonzalo, had distinguished himself in the wars of Italy, under the "Great Captain," Gonsalvo de Cordova; but he besmirched his family scutcheon by his amours with common women, and of his five sons could boast of but one who was legitimate.

Francisco was born in poverty and disgrace, though his father lived in Truxillo as a haughty *hidalgo*, and it is a tradition that even his mother neglected him, his life being saved by the nursing he received from a sow. At all events, his earliest recollections were of the swine among which he was reared and to the care of which his youth was devoted. He served as a swineherd until he had become a youth of goodly size, when his father took him to the Italian wars. He perceived that Francisco was a fighter; but he seems to have done nothing to advance his son from the ranks, and of his life as a soldier in Italy very little is known.

Accustomed from babyhood to cuffs and blows, neglect and hardship, and always with the curse of his birth upon him, Francisco seems to have led a hopeless sort of existence – at least ambitionless. No one had ever taken any interest in him, not even his mother, and though there were good schools in Truxillo, he grew up without learning either to read or to write. He never learned, in fact, for though he once or twice attempted it in after life, he soon gave up in disgust. He was certainly obtuse and pig-headed, though he had sense enough to perceive, when arrived at man's estate, that there was no fortune for either a swineherd or a soldier in Old Spain, and that to obtain one he must strike out in the new land discovered by Columbus beyond the Atlantic Ocean.

Cortés had preceded him by several years, but they must have met in Santo Domingo, for it is a matter of history that the former came near going with Ojeda's expedition in 1510, when we have the first positive evidence of Pizarro being in the West Indies. At the point from which Ojeda's expedition started – the south coast of Santo Domingo – the paths of Cortés and Pizarro diverged, for the former, prevented from embarking by illness, was saved for Cuba and the conquest of Mexico; while the latter, as we have seen, was making his devious way towards Peru and the west coast of South America.

Chance – blind chance – seems to have led these two young Spaniards towards their great careers, into which they stumbled as creatures of circumstance, impelled only by their courage, obstinacy, and constancy of purpose. At the outset of their New-World careers, however, neither had any hope of preferment beyond a captaincy; neither had definite views as to his future.

Cortés, when in Santo Domingo and Cuba, rather inclined to agriculture, especially as he could carry it on without personal labor, having received grants of Indians from the government; but Pizarro, after he abandoned his swine, seems never to have pursued any other vocation than that of the soldier. As a soldier we first find him in America; as a soldier he lived; a soldier he died.

Pizarro first heard of Peru, it is believed, when on that famous expedition which resulted in the discovery of the Pacific. Balboa was its commander, Pizarro a faithful captain, or lieutenant, in that perilous adventure. The cacique who had told them of the mountain whence they could view the ocean also told them of a great kingdom extending from its shores to the crests of the mighty Andes, but which would require more men to conquer than Balboa had with him then. More than a thousand men, he had asserted, even clad in armor, riding fiery steeds, and bearing the weapons that "spit forth smoke and lightning," would be necessary to reduce the powerful nation that occupied the Pacific slopes of the Andes.

Balboa took fire at the suggestion, and bent his energies towards accomplishing the subjugation of those unknown people – the Peruvians – of whom the cacique informed him. He, as commander, dominant man in Darien, was, of course, entitled to lead, to raise an expedition, to reap the glory of a conquest. These facts the obscure and plodding Pizarro recognized and assented to, though in his mind pondering the information received. Never for a moment, perhaps, did he entertain the thought that he might be commander of that expedition. But if he did he cleverly dissembled; at all events, he gave no sign that ambition stirred him, but performed his duties faithfully, as became the good soldier that he was.

Balboa had "taken possession" of the great "South Sea," the Pacific, by cutting down trees, erecting crosses, and piling up stones, in the name of King Ferdinand. Then he sent a body of men under Pizarro to find a trail to the coast. This was accomplished, and then he himself went down and made possession more actual by wading into the water up to his thighs. Brandishing his sword and shield, he called upon his men to witness that he thereby took possession of the great "South Sea" for the King of Spain, which, vast as it was, he pledged himself to defend against all the king's enemies.

An earnest of the riches the coast could yield was made manifest in a present to Balboa by Tumaco, an Indian chief, of golden ornaments and pearls to the number of two hundred and forty. The pearls had been injured by fire; but the Spaniards were shown the isles where others were to be found, and soon their losses were repaired.

Cacique Tumaco conveyed to them vague information of the great kingdom down the coast, and his words were treasured by Pizarro, as well as by Balboa, who resolved upon an expedition in search of it as soon as his circumstances would allow. With his wonted energy, he hastened back to the Darien shore, though so ill that he had to be borne in a litter by Indians, and set himself to prepare for the great undertaking. He also sent a messenger to Spain with the wonderful tidings that at last the "South Sea" had been found, though as yet no passage to it from the Caribbean. While this messenger was on his way with rich gifts of gold for the king, as well as the news (itself of the highest importance), things were happening in Spain which boded ill for Balboa. A governor of Darien had been appointed, an elderly man named Pedro Arias de Avila, generally known to the history of his times as Pedrarias. He sailed for his post with a large fleet filled with soldiers and adventurers, to the number of fifteen hundred, and arrived at Darien the last of June, 1514. Balboa had under him about one-third as many men as Pedrarias had brought; but they were all seasoned veterans, and he felt confident that, if so minded, he could prevent the new governor from landing. He was moved to do so, because, in the first place, he had come to supersede him, and in the second had brought back the lawyer Enciso, who bore no goodwill for Balboa, the man who had deprived him of command and sent him home to Spain.

But the new governor was welcomed by the veterans, including Balboa (who now had a force to reckon with beyond his strength), and was informed of all that had been done. He was also given descriptions of the places containing gold and pearls, and probably told of the rumors respecting the golden kingdom, since ascertained to be that of Peru.

Now, Pedrarias was crafty, haughty, and crabbed, and the wonder is that with these qualities he succeeded in controlling such desperate adventurers as the men of Darien. The most desperate of them, he knew, was Vasco Nuñez de Balboa, and he resolved to rid himself of this rival, who had performed all the great deeds, while he himself held the power and had done nothing.

If Balboa had not been so active and enterprising, but content, like Pizarro, to hold a subordinate position until the chances were good for securing a higher, by the king's favor, he might have saved his honors and his head. As it was, through having seized upon the leadership when Enciso commanded, he incurred the ill-will of Pedrarias, who committed that crime which, by linking his name with that of Balboa, constitutes his chief claim to fame. Before committing that crime, however, he was destined to experience the terrible effects of fever and famine, which, combined, carried away seven hundred of his colonists. These were all new men, for the veterans were proof against disease as well as inured to hunger and privation.

It is not on record that Pizarro suffered from any disease, except such as was brought upon him by his indiscretions, nor that he was wounded in his many encounters with the Indians. He bore, if not a charmed life, one exempt from the penalties which other and better men were paying for wandering into a wilderness until that time unvisited by white men since the creation of the world.

Having become jealous of Balboa, Pedrarias refused to send him out on expeditions, even over his own routes of discovery, and, as he was not fit to go himself, he appointed his cousin, a man named Morales, to go in his stead. Morales proved as inefficient as Pedrarias, and as they could not, or would not, trust Balboa, Pizarro was sent as second in command, but, by reason of his skill and knowledge of the country, virtually became the leader. Under his guidance the first exploring party sent out by Pedrarias reached the Pacific shores and embarked in canoes for a group of islands which had been pointed out to Pizarro by the Indians as abounding in pearls. The natives of these islands fought the Spaniards fiercely; but they were driven inland, and on the shores of the islands were found so many and such beautiful pearls that Pedrarias, on the return of the expedition, resolved to remove the seat of government from Darien to the opposite coast. There he founded the city of Panama, which, with San Miguel Gulf (discovered by Balboa) and the "Pearl Islands" (first exploited and named by Pizarro), may be found to-day on a map of the isthmus and its waters.

Terrible atrocities were committed by Morales, the nominal leader of the pearl-hunters, who massacred hundreds of Indians and threw the captured caciques to his blood-hounds. On the return march, finding himself hard pressed by avenging Indians under a cacique named Birú, Morales stabbed his captives at frequent intervals, and left their mangled bodies in the trails. This was in order to detain the pursuers, who, more humane than the white fiends, were constrained to pause and give the remains of their friends or relatives burial.

Whether Morales was led, or merely seconded, by Pizarro, is not known; but doubtless both were engaged in the atrocious work of murdering inoffensive natives merely because they possessed gold and jewels, which the Spaniards desired.

This was but one of several expeditions sent out by Pedrarias, in all of which combined – according to a monk who accompanied some of them – more than forty thousand Indians were destroyed, "killed by the sword, or thrown to savage dogs."

It seems incredible that so many human lives should have been sacrificed, merely to gratify the lusts of savage men who had no claim whatever to the territory they invaded nor any right to coerce its inhabitants. But, whether forty thousand were destroyed or only a few hundred, the fact that the lives of the natives were held of no account shows the disposition of the conquerors. That they were consistently cruel, barbarous, more savage than the so-called "savages" themselves, cannot be gainsaid; and the most relentless of them all was the subject of this narrative, Francisco Pizarro.

Few of them lived long to enjoy their ill-gotten, blood-stained treasures; most of them perished miserably, victims of violence, and the first of this rapacious company to fall was then the most conspicuous – perhaps not the most blameworthy – Vasco Nuñez de Balboa. He had incurred the enmity of Pedrarias by aspiring to command, for which he was so eminently fitted, and it was charged by the governor that he intended to usurp his power. Still, with a cunning as despicable as it was deep, Pedrarias had enchained Balboa by bestowing upon him the hand of his daughter in marriage. The young lady was then in Spain; but at Darien was the cacique's daughter, beloved of Balboa, and herein lay a fruitful source of trouble, which we will not discuss. Pretending to accede to Balboa's desire for active service, the vicious Pedrarias allowed him to build some brigantines on the Caribbean coast of the isthmus, which, after incredible toils, were transported piecemeal overland to the Pacific. The natives did most of the work, under the supervision of Balboa; but he himself suffered terribly, at one time being reduced to the verge of starvation and compelled to subsist upon roots and leaves. But his heroic endeavors to placate the governor and form a fleet in which to escape his persecutions, were unavailing. As soon as the last brigantine had been forwarded over the mountains, from the wild port of Acla, in which the timbers were shaped and fitted, the governor sent a company of soldiers to arrest him. An *alguacil mayor*, Enciso, accompanied the soldiers, and it may have been at his instigation that the deed was performed, for he had a grudge of long standing against Balboa; but the captain of the company had nothing of the sort. He was, in fact, until the arrival of Pedrarias, Balboa's right-hand man and boon companion, hitherto his faithful adherent, for it was none other than Pizarro, who captained that band of soldiers. When Balboa saw him, and divined the purport of his coming, he exclaimed, reproachfully: "What is this, Francisco? You were not wont to come out in this fashion to receive me!" But he made no resistance, and was escorted to Darien, where, charges having been preferred against him by a licentiate in the pay of Pedrarias, this father-in-law of Balboa sentenced him to death!

The sentence was unjust, and Balboa protested his innocence; but there was no appeal. It was carried out the very day it was pronounced, and a public crier preceded the governor's victim to the scaffold, proclaiming, so that all might hear: "This is the justice which our lord the King and Pedrarias his representative, in his name, commands to be done to this man, as a traitor and usurper of the lands subject to the royal crown!"

And this man, this "traitor and usurper," though he had made a discovery scarcely second to that made by Columbus, was dragged through the streets like a common malefactor, and publicly beheaded. This was Balboa's reward for too faithfully serving an ungrateful king.

As his head rolled to the ground, after having been severed from his body by the keen axe of the executioner, it was seized and placed upon a pole erected for the purpose in the public square. The vengeance of Pedrarias was not satisfied even with this, for the remains of Balboa were dishonored, as were those of the four companions beheaded with him, and their properties were confiscated.

The people who swarmed the square were aghast, dismayed, their lamentations filled the air; but they dared not intercede, for the governor had surrounded the scaffold with soldiers, and they were commanded by one who always obeyed the orders of his superior, Captain Francisco Pizarro!

III

SAILING THE UNKNOWN SEA

1524

WHAT were the thoughts of Pizarro, as he gazed upon Balboa's gory trunk and beheld the head of that once-valiant commander roll to the ground? If his sluggish brain conceived any ideas at all, the thought which was uppermost must have related in some way to the removal of a rival from his path. He may have felt resentful towards Pedrarias for his dastardly act, but he was too politic to show it, and his nature was too debased, his sensibilities too blunt, for him to feel the horror and injustice of it all.

He still did his duty as a soldier, and Pedrarias had no more faithful adherent, thenceforth, than Francisco Pizarro. His behavior during the terrible retreat across the isthmus made by Morales, when, hemmed in by prowling savages, he had again and again charged upon the foe, holding them at bay while his companions effected a temporary escape from death, had commended him to the irascible old governor. He had been virtually the leader of that forlorn expedition, which had returned so rich in gold and pearls, yet so decimated by death, and by all he was acknowledged to have been its savior from absolute destruction.

He was the man, of all men then on the isthmus, to take the place made vacant by the death of Balboa; but, though he might have carried on that leader's work, have manned the brigantines, and sailed southwardly in quest of the shadowy kingdom of which the cacique had informed him, he then had no opportunity. For, though he had displayed great ability as a fighter, he had not given evidence of possessing the qualities that make for supreme command. Perhaps he was too wary to do so, knowing the jealous nature of the governor, and preferred to bide his time – which might come after the removal, by death or otherwise, of Pedrarias. He awaited this event, however, in vain for years. The crafty old man had a strong hold on life, and before he was superseded caused more than Balboa and his companions to lose their heads. He sent Espinosa, the man who had prosecuted Balboa, to refit and man the ships the latter had built and experimentally navigated; but he took the wrong direction, sailing northward instead of southward, and returned without having accomplished anything. In his heart, Pizarro was delighted at this turn of affairs, but he dared not voice his thoughts.

Within two years after the execution of Balboa, or in 1519, Pedrarias removed the seat of government across the isthmus to Panama, and, after various excursions of a military character for his master into Nicaragua, Pizarro settled down to the life of a cattle farmer. He had won distinction as a *conquistador*, having then been ten years engaged in fighting Indians, founding colonies, and, to the best of his ability, serving his king. That he had also served himself, and had accumulated quite a fortune from his years of toil and hardship, is nothing to his discredit. In truth, it is rather strange than otherwise that he should have saved anything at all, since the Spanish adventurers were thriftless, given to gambling, and reckless of the future. Perhaps, however, Pizarro was a better gambler, as well as more provident, than the others. Certain it is that soon after the founding of Panama he held a large acreage of land in its vicinity, which he worked, or made pretence of working, with a *repartimiento* of Indian slaves.

But, as already mentioned, he was not the stuff of which farmers and planters are made. First, last, and all the time he was a soldier; and, moreover, there lingered with him the remembrance of the Peruvian tradition. Finally, he imparted his information to his partner, one Almagro, who, like himself, was a soldier of fortune. Like Pizarro, he was born out of wedlock – a foundling; like him, also, he was stained with crime, having fled to the New World in his youth on account of having stabbed a companion.

Almagro was told of the land of gold, with its temples supposed to be filled with treasures, the dominions of its ruler filled with teeming millions; of the strange beasts, the llamas, drawings of which he had seen, but which as yet no white men had ever beheld. Almagro listened and wondered. He was the exact opposite of his partner, for, while the latter was sluggish, grasping and covetous, silent and reserved, he was active in mind and body, and generous to a fault. He became enthusiastic over the scheme which, having long dwelled upon it in his mind, Pizarro slowly unfolded, and was for setting forth at once in search of the land of wonders.

Pizarro was not sure the time had come for that. Provided, in the first place, they could obtain the consent of the governor, they would receive no assistance from that grasping individual; in the second, therefore, they must furnish their own funds, and they had not yet accumulated enough for the venture. In this emergency they bethought themselves of an individual who was on terms of friendship with both, and withal a man of talents as well as substance. This man was Fernando de Luque, a *clerigo*, or ecclesiastic, attached to the cathedral of Panama, and on an intimate footing with the governor. Having been cautiously broached on the subject, after some thought he consented to enter the partnership, and thus the "triumvirate" was formed which eventually accomplished – at least, it led up to – the conquest of Peru.

Pedrarias was insanely jealous of his prerogatives, and more crabbed than ever; but the clerigo managed him so carefully that he finally consented to the scheme, with the provision – which they had anticipated – of receiving a fourth part of the profits. In this manner the strange partnership was formed, consisting of two soldiers, one cleric, and the governor of Panama, who, though a "silent" partner, inasmuch as he did not contribute any funds, had greater power than any of the others to make or mar the expedition. This compact was concluded in 1522, at a time when the glorious news from Cortés in Mexico was stirring the souls of men in Panama and elsewhere; and this "cousin" of Cortés, Pizarro, may have been moved thereby to break the spell which had so long held him and to imitate his exploits. The partnership continued, in a manner, during several years; but at last, as will be narrated in course, Pizarro became the sole survivor of the company.

Pedrarias, filled as he was with the venom of distrust and jealousy, could not grasp the situation in its immensity, but frittered away his time in little ventures into Nicaragua, finally, in 1526, going off on a head-hunting expedition there on the trail of a lieutenant whom he imagined disloyal. This unfortunate, an hidalgo named De Cordova, was the first to meet the conquerors of Mexico coming down from the north, through Honduras, and doubtless might have accomplished great things, had not Pedrarias cut short his career by taking off his head.

An incentive to the formation of the triumvirate probably lay in the unsuccessful voyage made in 1522 by one Andagoya, who, in the brigantines Balboa had built, coasted farther to the south than any one before him, merely confirming the reports of a rich country concealed behind the mountains, whose glittering crests, covered with eternal snows, he had ventured far enough to see. The wonder is, not that this partnership was formed, but that some others did not make their way along the southern coast.

Nine years had passed since Balboa and Pizarro first looked upon the Pacific; Panama and the "Golden Castile" on the isthmus had lured hundreds of cavaliers to their death; but there still remained many adventurers, young, reckless, and filled with longings to emulate Cortés and Columbus. Why, then, was it left for three men well advanced in years to form this compact for conquest? Pizarro and Almagro were over fifty years of age, while De Luque was a staid priest of Panama, whose departure in this instance, from his regular course of life earned for him the sobriquet the public bestowed of *Fernando el Loco* or the "Crazy -head." He was the moneyed man of the enterprise; Pizarro was to be the chief adventurer, fighter, and discoverer; while Almagro was to act as go-between, remaining at Panama to beat up recruits and forward supplies.

Two years elapsed before their preparations for a voyage were complete, and it was not until November 14, 1524, that Pizarro finally set sail from the port of Panama. The funds of the partners were not sufficient to fit out a large fleet, so two small vessels merely had been purchased. The larger of the two was one of the brigantines built by the lamented Balboa. It had lain dismantled in the harbor for years, and was hardly fit for sea-service; but in it Pizarro embarked, with a hundred men, more or less, which Almagro, after infinite exertions, had drummed up in Panama.

Previous to the departure from port a solemn service was held in the cathedral, at which the prominent figures were the three partners, Almagro, Pizarro, and De Luque the priest. They partook of the sacrament together, at the instance of the clerigo, who divided the holy water into three parts, and the compact between the three was recited and renewed in the most impressive manner. The cathedral was crowded with the motley populace of Panama, and after the ceremony was over a procession was formed, led by Pizarro and Pedrarias, followed by the soldiers and sailors, after whom trooped a shouting multitude.

The Panamans had derided the venture of "Fernando el Loco" and his partners, but now that the long-exploited voyage was really about to begin, they went wild with enthusiasm. They wept over the leave-taking of the four principals in the affair, as embraces and caresses were exchanged between them; they fired salutes from cannon and arquebuses, as Pizarro and his men went aboard their vessel, and as it finally swept out of the bay towards the open ocean. Now that the expedition was an accomplished fact, the people of Panama, who had ridiculed the idea, realized how great were the faith and constancy of those who had promoted it. The least they could do was to grant their approval, and this was given so heartily that Pizarro, standing upon the high after-cabin of his ship, repeatedly removed his great, plumed hat and bowed his acknowledgments.

So the adventurers went off in a "blaze of glory," and for a time were filled with satisfaction; but not many days passed ere murmurings began. Almagro, in his desire to complete the complement of soldiers and sailors for the voyage, had impressed every vagabond he had found running loose in Panama, as well as hired all the good men – which latter were quite few. Thus, while Panama was well rid of its vagabonds, Pizarro found himself encumbered with such a pack of graceless wretches as any commander less forceful than he would have turned back into the purlieus whence they were drawn. Not so Francisco Pizarro, however. The old soldier was in his element when in command of refractory men. He neither bullied nor beat them ; but he awed them into submission just the same, and they were compelled to sail forthwith him into the unknown.

He shaped his course for the Pearl Islands, the scene of his adventures ten years before, where he had formerly found most beautiful pearls in abundance, and to which he had given the name by which they are still known. Having taken in wood and water there, he crossed the open mouth of gulf San Miguel, the shores of which he and Balboa had explored in 1513, and on the waters of which they had embarked with the Indian cacique in canoes. Thence he coasted southward to the headland of Puerto Pinas, which was the farthest point reached by Andagoya, and, entering the mouth of a small river beyond this promontory, made a landing on the verge of a forest.

He was now in a region which had never been explored, for no white man had gone farther than Andagoya, despite the eleven years that had elapsed since Balboa's great discovery. Feeling it incumbent upon him to investigate thoroughly as he went on, Pizarro resolved to explore the little river, perchance there might be gold-mines, or a settlement, at its mouth or along its banks. It was called the Birú, and the similarity of this name to that of the land of which the adventurers were in search – Peru – gave them the impression that it could not be far away. But, notwithstanding his auspicious beginning, and in spite of the thorough preparation he had made for the voyage, months, even years, were to glide by ere he was to look upon the riches of Peru. Nothing was found along the river indicating a populous country, or one abounding in natural wealth, so the explorers were recalled, and the ship dropped down-stream to the sea, where the southerly course was resumed. After some days and nights of voyaging, another lonely inlet was descried, and an anchorage was made; but this place proved as desolate and repellent as Birú, and after wood and water had been obtained the open sea was sought again. Ten days of aimless sailing succeeded, during which the voyagers were assailed by tempests so severe that the crazy craft was strained in every part. The wind blew fiercely, always ahead, the seas ran mountains high, and at last, worn out with continual watching and working, Pizarro resolved to return to the inlet last entered. As the provisions began to fail at this point, and the hapless Argonauts were finally reduced to an allowance of two ears of Indian-corn a day, with an occasional bite of green cowhide and some palm-tree buds, they called the place *Puerto de la Hambre* (Hungry Harbor). The country adjacent appeared to them the most desolate spot in the world, for, while dense, tropical forest hemmed them in, the shores were steep and rocky, and nothing life-supporting could be found anywhere.

The rains still fell incessantly, the dank forest was all but impenetrable, the scant provisions were daily growing less, so Pizarro concluded to send back to the Pearl Islands for fresh supplies. His men were for returning, nearly all of them, but to this he would not consent. It was with difficulty that he hushed their murmurings, overcame their mutinous feelings, and finally despatched the vessel to the islands. It was under the command of an officer named Montenegro, who promised that he would perform his duty faithfully and make all haste to secure the needed provisions and return.

Two weeks were allowed him, that time being considered ample for the voyage; but thrice two weeks passed away before Pizarro saw his ship again, and meanwhile he lost thirty of his men by sickness and starvation. Even their scant supply of corn gave out, and they were compelled to live on small shellfish and sea-weed, their last bit of cowhide being a strip of tanned leather from the ship's pump, which, boiled and divided among the starving men, was greedily devoured. It was thought that the coast was absolutely uninhabited, not a soul having been discovered on the voyage ; but one day, as some of these gaunt and haggard men were wandering in sheer desperation about the forest, they came upon a clearing in which was a group of Indian huts. They hastened with the welcome news to Pizarro, and soon all who could walk were on the way. The savages fled at sight of the white men, who lost no time in breaking into their huts, where they found ample supplies of corn and cocoa-nuts, to which they helped themselves without asking leave of the owners. These soon returned, impelled by curiosity, and, after they had overcome their fears, ventured to converse with the strangers by signs.

In his years of intercourse with the isthmian natives, Pizarro must have picked up some Indian words, which served him well at this time, for he received information from these people that their settlement was but an outpost of a mighty nation, as it were. Ten days' journey inland, beyond the cordilleras, lived the great king who ruled their world. He was called the "Child of the Sun." His empire was so vast that no one person had seen the whole of it, and his riches so abundant that no one could measure them.

An assurance that, at last, he was on the confines of the golden country was afforded Pizarro by the ornaments the Indians wore, which, though of rude workmanship, were of pure gold. The Spaniards were greatly rejoiced at this news direct from the land of gold, which had seemed so vague and unsubstantial hitherto. They now had the evidence of their ears and their eyes, that there was such a kingdom as had been described to Pizarro and Balboa, years before.

As for Pizarro himself, it is not known whether he manifested any emotion at receiving this confirmation of the cacique's story; but he probably used it to the best advantage in cheering the drooping spirits of his followers. It was the first positive information that had been received from the land of the Incas; but as it came filtered through sign-language mainly, it might have been misinterpreted.

Returning to the coast with the provisions afforded by their timely discovery, the Spaniards resumed their watch for Montenegro's vessel; but their corn and cocoa-nuts were exhausted, and starvation was again staring them in the face, before their eyes were cheered by the sight of a sail. Seven long weeks, in fact, passed by before the ship returned, and by this time most of them were so weak they could scarcely stand.

As soon, however, as his men had somewhat recovered their strength, Pizarro hoisted sail again and resumed his interrupted voyage. They then had provisions ample for a time, and the sight of native gold had whetted their appetites, so at first there were few protests against proceeding farther. Favored at first by good weather, they proceeded rapidly down the coast, and eventually reached a region where the sea-shore was more open than hitherto. Perceiving signs of human occupancy there, Pizarro concluded to land and establish a station. Penetrating the fringe of mangroves along the shore, where the stilted trees were pierced by waterways or avenues, the Spaniards saw on a hill, less than a league distant, a palisaded village. It seemed to be deserted, so they took possession, and were delighted to find it well provisioned, and supplied as well with gold, in nuggets and ornaments. It seemed strange to Pizarro, acquainted as he was with Indian wiles, that there should be no people in or near it, so he sent Montenegro with a small force to investigate the forest adjacent.

But these Indians were more wary and warlike than any he had encountered on that coast. They had left their village as a bait to attract the invaders, but were watching their movements from the forest. No sooner, therefore, was Montenegro's force out of sight among the defiles of the hills than a body of warriors sprang from ambush near the village and sent a shower of arrows into the ranks of Pizarro's company. Three soldiers were killed outright, and many wounded, despite their coats of mail and quilted cotton. Possessing great contempt for the natives, the result of many conflicts with them on the isthmus, Pizarro sallied forth to meet them in the open. He was ably supported by his men, but, recognized by the Indians as the leader, upon him was concentrated such a storm of darts and arrows that he was seven times wounded and compelled to retreat. Pizarro always kept his face to the foe, and as he was slowly retreating backward, holding his buckler as a defence and stabbing at the foremost assailants with his sword, his foot slipped on the slope of the hill and he fell to the ground. In an instant a mob of savages was upon him, but, throwing them aside, he sprang to his feet, and slashed about him so vigorously that they were put to flight, after two had been cut down by his sword. His men rallied to the rescue, and at the same time Montenegro attacked the Indians in the rear, so that they were thrown into confusion and retreated into the forest, where they disappeared. The hill-slope was covered with their dead and wounded; but, as the Spaniards also had suffered severely, they concluded to evacuate the place, which they did after plundering the houses, and fell back upon their ship.

It had been Pizarro's intention to send the ship back to Panama, while he awaited fresh provisions and reinforcements at this place, which he called Quemado; but the attack, most fortunately, had been made in time for him to countermand the order, else his force might have been exterminated. Despite his losses, however, he was not disposed to complain, for this desperate attack had given him a foretaste of what was to be expected farther on, as he should penetrate the country, and he fully realized the inadequacy of his little force to attempt its conquest. Still, the idea of returning to Panama was so repugnant to him that, rather than face his creditors, a bankrupt adventurer, he caused himself and a portion of his crew to be set on shore at Chicamá, on the main-land to the westward of the port whence he had sailed, and there awaited further news from Almagro and his friends.

His wounds soon healed, for, unfortunately for the southern Indians, they were not acquainted with the use of poisoned arrows. Still, these wounds inflicted at Quemado were the first he had received in many years, if not the first of consequence in his experience, and probably made a lasting impression. He must have been convinced of the futility of proceeding farther, unless better equipped than he had been on this first expedition. He had no intention, however, of abandoning his project, and so grimly waited at Chicamá, while the treasurer of the expedition proceeded with the vessel to Panama, carrying with him a full account of what had been done, together with the gold that had been collected. Governor Pedrarias was furious when he learned of the terrible losses, especially of the lives that had been spent in this wild-goose chase after an unknown empire. He swore that he desired nothing better than to get Pizarro into his clutches; and as for allowing him to set forth again, wasting precious treasure and shedding the blood of his cavaliers, the heavens should fall before he would consent to it!

Pizarro was careful not to place himself in the power of the murderous Pedrarias, for he remembered Balboa. But he was still determined to carry on his researches, inflexibly bent upon achieving the conquest of Peru, and no man on earth, not even Pedrarias, should turn him from his purpose.

IV

THE DESPERATE ADVENTURER

1526-1528

IT was no consolation for Pizarro to learn that, while he was on his return voyage, Almagro was seeking him in the south, and that they were playing a game of cross-purposes. Yet such was the case. His faithful partner, after again raking and scraping the environs of Panama, as with a fine-tooth comb, had raised a scurvy crew of soldier-sailors, and, fitting up the second vessel they had purchased, had sailed in search of him down the coast.

He barely missed him several times, at last arriving at Quemado, where Pizarro had received such a warm reception. The natives had returned to their village, and behind the palisades awaited the coming of the strangers. No gold was to be found, as it had been taken away by Pizarro, but Almagro resolved to attack the place, nevertheless. He assailed it with fury, and eventually drove out its defenders; but he fared still worse than Pizarro, whose wounds were not severe, as he was wounded in the head by a javelin and lost the sight of an eye.

He narrowly escaped with his life, and the pain from his wound was great, yet he persevered in his search, sailing farther south than any one before him, and turning about at the river San Juan, where he found a large Indian settlement and lands in a high state of cultivation.

Having landed at different points along the coast, when on the way thither, Almagro contrived to secure considerable treasure, so his voyage was not altogether bootless, though personally he had suffered severely. Touching at the Pearl Islands on his way back, he learned that Pizarro was then in hiding at Chicamá, and, seeking him out, had the satisfaction of finding him still in health, and with about fifty stout comrades still faithful to their cause. They embraced with fervor, and then, after recounting their adventures, mutually resolved to continue their explorations.

The old governor was still obdurate, but finally De Luque, the clerigo, won him over; though, with malicious cunning, he insisted that Almagro should accompany the second expedition and have equal command with Pizarro. This condition, as he craftily intended, made trouble, by exciting the suspicions of Pizarro, who was disposed to believe that Almagro had solicited the command himself. Up to this time the three friends had worked in harmony for the success of their schemes. De Luque had furnished the funds, Almagro had toiled night and day to fit out, arm, provision, and man the vessels, while Pizarro had not spared himself nor his crew in his endeavors to insure success.

Pedrarias did all he could to cripple the enterprise and to excite distrust in the minds of the two chief adventurers. They were soon to see the last of him, but before he was superseded he shot a "Parthian arrow" at them, in the demand for an accounting. He proposed to retire from the partnership, and demanded, as his share of the spoils, four thousand pesos. He finally accepted a thousand, and, after much grumbling and many threats as to what he would do to Pizarro when once he had him again in Panama, he allowed the original trio to continue their explorations.

Almagro sailed from Panama at last, with two ships, better fitted for the voyage than before, and with a force of one hundred and sixty men. He gave the command of one ship to Pizarro, retaining the other for himself. Previous to setting out, the contract entered into by the partners was reaffirmed in the same solemn manner as before, each one taking oath, "in the name of God and the holy Evangelists," to be true to the others. Whatever might result from the enterprise, even to the extent of a kingdom or an empire, with the captives and their ransoms, was to be divided equally. This they mutually promised and swore to, calling upon God to take vengeance upon them if they failed to comply with the provisions of the contract.

This instrument was dated March 10, 1526, and received the signatures of Pizarro and Almagro by proxy, as one of these worthies was absent, and neither of them could write. So affecting was the ceremonial which took place, as before, in the great cathedral, that many of the spectators were "moved to tears"; yet the two commanders were scarcely afloat upon the ocean ere the slumbering flame of distrust broke forth. Subsequently, they almost came to blows, and in the end one of them lost his life, virtually at the hands of the other.

Afloat at last, however, with two good ships, some good men, a few horses, and munitions, Almagro and Pizarro steered straight for the river San Juan, arrived at which they threw off the mask of friendship assumed on former occasions and promptly attacked the natives. In one of the towns along the banks of the river they captured several Indians, and booty to the amount of fifteen thousand pesos in gold. This plunder, so quickly obtained, determined them on a course of action which shows the wisdom and energy of the leaders. Knowing that the sight of it would create a profound impression in Panama, and probably draw recruits to their cause, it was resolved that Almagro should at once return and endeavour to obtain such recruits, while the pilot of the expedition, in the other ship, should proceed southward on an exploring trip merely, without engaging in hostilities.

Each was to return as speedily as possible, after his purpose was achieved, and report to Pizarro, who, with the bulk of the soldiery, was to remain on or near the coast. It was a wild, a desperate scheme, and one only to be thought of by desperate adventurers, for, according to reports from the natives, they were then on the verge of a populous country, the warlike natives of which could easily sweep away, by concerted effort, any small band of invaders like this, even though encased in steel and armed with wonderful weapons. But the voyagers sailed off, Almagro to the north and Ruiz, the pilot, to the south, leaving Pizarro and his men alone in the enemies' country.

It was not long before this isolated band of Spaniards was enduring the pangs of hunger, and Pizarro 's old enemy, starvation, looked him in the face again. For himself, seemingly, Pizarro did not care; he was used to privation, even laughed at famine. By his patient endurance, tact, sympathy, and never-ceasing attentions, he won the regard of his men, and kept their spirits up until

Ruiz, the pilot, returned with most wonderful stories of what he had seen on the southward voyage. He had not only discovered cities and towns occupied by people far advanced in civilization, but had seen and overhauled a large native boat, by the Indians called a *balsa*, which contained a cargo that might have come from the Spice Islands.

The balsa, of itself, was a wonderful craft, being the first ever found, owned by natives of America, navigated by means of a sail. It was a large double raft, with thatched huts on its decks, containing bales of cloths delicate in texture and exquisite in coloring, beautiful pottery, and articles in gold, together with scales in which to weigh the precious metal and gems. Conversing with the owners of the balsa by means of signs, Ruiz had learned of a land beyond, which abounded in temples and palaces, and the capital of which, called Cuzco, was the home of Huayna Capac, their king. The mountains contained rich veins of silver and mines of gold, while the hills were covered with their native sheep, by them called llamas, from the wool of which the cloths composing their gaments were woven. They themselves came from the coast town of Tumbez, which, though a place of importance, could not compare with the capital.

Ruiz had met with people prepared to fight him, but, as his instructions were to explore, and not to engage in conflict with the natives, he had avoided close contact with them, and had thus returned without having shed human blood, and with little plunder. It is refreshing to read of an expedition like this one conducted by sturdy Bartholomew Ruiz, a native of Moguer, the little town near Palos, in Spain, which produced the Pinzons, who befriended and sailed with Columbus. His townsman and exemplar, Vicente Yañez Pinzon, was the first European to cross the equator on the Atlantic coast of South America, and Ruiz has the distinction of being the first to pass south of the line on the Pacific; though Magellan had first crossed it sailing northwardly, in 1520.

While the pilot was absent, Pizarro and his band had endured incredible sufferings, mainly from hunger and sickness. Clouds of mosquitoes had made them miserable, *caimans*, or alligators, had devoured some of the Spaniards, and fourteen had lost their lives in attacks by the natives. Still, Pizarro was undaunted, and when, a few days after the arrival of Ruiz, Almagro returned with provisions and a reinforcement of eighty soldiers, he immediately re-embarked his men.

All were now in good spirits, with a prospect of leaving the scenes of their sufferings behind them, and a lure of gold and gems to lead them on. But the winds and sea -currents turned against them, tempests arose and buffeted them sorely, and they were compelled to seek a haven. This they found in a natural harbor of an island which had been discovered by Ruiz and by him called Gallo. Here they remained a fortnight, engaged in recruiting their strength and repairing their vessels, which the gales had racked severely. Then they went on again, and passing over to the main-land arrived off the port of Tacamez, a town of two thousand dwellings arranged along regular streets, which were filled with people, whose golden ornaments glittered in the sunshine. Two rivers coursed through a verdant and highly cultivated plain, one of which, Pizarro was told by some captives aboard, flowed over golden sands, while the other was famous for its brilliant emeralds.

The country was evidently richer than any other the Spaniards had seen; but even so, its inhabitants knew how to defend it, for a flotilla of war-canoes came out to meet the ships, with golden ensigns at their prows, while a force estimated at ten thousand warriors marched along the shore, seeking an opportunity to engage the enemy at close quarters. This opportunity the dauntless Pizarro was disposed to give them ; but, landing with a force of mailed soldiers for the purpose, he was soon surrounded by an overwhelming number of warriors. They were well armed, too, and pressed him and his small company so hard that they were in danger of being driven into the sea, if not entirely annihilated, when they were saved as if by a miracle. That is, if we may believe the story told by the Spaniards, a miracle in guise of an accident saved them. Some of the horses had been landed, the cavaliers had mounted, and were preparing to charge the assembled hosts, when one of them fell from his charger. The Indians had never seen a horse before, and like others of their race, as in Mexico, thought steed and rider formed one animal. When, therefore, this strange animal fell apart, they were more astonished than at sight of the original apparition, and, opening their ranks, allowed the Spaniards to regain their ships.

Whether this really happened or not, it is certain that even such doughty fighters as Almagro and Pizarro deemed it best not to attack this horde of barbarians, after experiencing the nature of the reception they had prepared for them, and at a council of war, aboard ship, resolved upon retracing their course to the island of Gallo. Neither of the captains was prepared to abandon the expedition entirely, but both were convinced that to proceed farther, with their incomplete equipment, would be the height of folly. The question now arose as to which one should remain and which proceed to Panama for reinforcements. Pizarro held that he should be allowed to make the voyage while Almagro remained behind, for it was hardly fair that the latter should have all the pleasuring, careering about in a ship or loitering at home, while he, Pizarro, should undergo the toil and suffering.

His partner held otherwise, arguing that he had the requisite experience in obtaining recruits and supplies, and, moreover, that, although Pedrarias was now superseded by another governor, he still had influence enough to "lay Pizarro by the heels" and cast him into a dungeon. If both went back without having accomplished anything worth while, there was a certainty that their creditors would incarcerate them forthwith, in default of the treasure which they had hoped to receive for their advances. This was the only thing upon which they agreed.

The dispute waxed so warm that each laid his hand on his sword, and but for the interference of Ruiz, and Ribera the king's treasurer, there might have been an encounter. Both were good swordsmen, both were valiant and obstinate, so there was little doubt that one or both would have been slain. But, while Almagro was of powerful build, he was short and "squatty," and lacked the "reach" of his antagonist, Pizarro, who was tall, broad-shouldered, and as agile as ever he had been in the best days of his soldiering.

In passing, we may as well mention that, of the two, Pizarro more nearly approached the ideal leader and commander, being handsome, energetic, and unsparing of himself on tedious march, or in action with the enemy. Almagro, however, though hideously ugly and afflicted with disease, was equally brave, and had the reputation of being more generous and companionable than his rival.

A truce was patched up between the two, and after his blood had cooled, Pizarro consented to remain at Gallo, while Almagro returned to Panama for another foray upon its resources. As all the soldiers also wished to return, being heartily disgusted with the hard conditions by which they were oppressed, the two commanders were hardly able to restrain them. Prevented, not only from leaving the island with Almagro, but from sending home letters to their friends, these soldiers "kindled a fire in the rear" of their leaders by smuggling a note to Panama in a ball of cotton sent as a specimen product to the governor's wife. In this "round robin," signed by several of the soldiers, their woes were recited in doggerel verse, which, though rude and unpolished, became an effective weapon against Almagro and Pizarro. These two were compared to a drover and a butcher, the one going to Panama for victims, the other remaining at Gallo, but both engaged in slaughter:

"O good Lord Señor Governor,
Have pity on our woes;
The butcher stays behind with us,
To you the drover goes!"

The soldiers' verses, together with the haggard and emaciated appearance of the returning survivors, had such an effect upon the new governor, Pedro de los Rios, that he not only forbade the raising of more recruits, but at once despatched two vessels to Gallo for Pizarro and his men. They were under command of a lawyer named Tafur, who found the objects of his search in a famishing condition, their clothing in rags, their armor rusty and battered, and themselves dispirited to the last degree. They hailed the coming of Tafur with delight, and, after ravenously consuming the food he gave them, gladly consented to return with him to Panama. All, in fact, returned, save Pizarro and thirteen stout-hearted companions, who decided to remain with him and share the toils and dangers of another campaign. Various stories are told of the manner in which Pizarro persuaded these thirteen to remain with him, but that which has received credence from most historians is the following: He assembled his men on the strand, and, marking a line in the sand with his sword, stepped across it, saying: "On this side lies Peru, which is to be gained only by fatigue, hunger, thirst, and the facing of dangers untold; on the other is Panama, with its life of ease, but of poverty and obscurity. Choose ye, comrades, whether to go back with Tafur or remain with me; for I have no desire to force any man against his will."

It was a crisis in Pizarro 's life, and he met it boldly. Folding his arms across his breast, he stood proudly erect, and waited the decision of his comrades. He knew, and they knew, that no matter how many stayed behind, nothing could be done without further assistance from Panama; but this assistance was promised, by Almagro and the clerigo, provided Pizarro would hold on a little longer. It was the moral effect of the act, in refusing to abandon what had been gained, and holding to what had been achieved, that would enable them to win in the end.

At first, there was much murmuring among the company clustered together on the sands; then one of them turned suddenly and strode across the line to Pizarro 's side. It was Ruiz, the pilot, a man animated by high aspirations. He was soon joined by another, a Greek cavalier, Pedro of Candia, who afterwards became a shining figure in the conquest. Eleven others followed them, and that was all. Just a "baker's dozen" stayed by Pizarro, out of more than a hundred. The commander bit his lip, his eye flashed; but he uttered no word, either of reproach or commendation. He had his own reasons for remaining, and his comrades, he supposed, also had theirs; but he resolved that their constancy to him in his evil fortune should not go unrewarded. After they had crossed the line, and thus cast in their lot with his, not one of them went back;

except that the pilot, Ruiz, was sent with Tafur to aid Almagro in fitting out another expedition. The lawyer was provoked by the action of Pizarro and his sturdy twelve, and at first refused to give them any provisions, but finally relented, and then sailed away to the north, leaving them alone upon this desolate island.

Gallo was so very desolate, indeed, that the Spaniards concluded they could not exist upon it, so they constructed a raft (no vessel having been left them), and made their way to the isle of Gorgona, about seventy miles distant. They were several days in making the voyage, but when arrived at Gorgona found it high and wooded, with spring-fed streams coursing through thickets of tropical vegetation. As pheasants and rabbits were abundant here, which the Spaniards killed with their cross-bows, they did not lack for food at first ; but after these had become scarce, they were compelled to subsist upon such shell-fish as they could find, together with palm nuts and buds, They were not, however, brought to such extremities as at Quemado, though they often went hungry and suffered greatly from noxious insects.

It was a sort of Crusoe life that Pizarro and his twelve companions led at Gorgona, though they were not quite so solitary as Defoe's sailor castaway, whose adventures occurred about one hundred and forty years after their own. Seven months they lived isolated from all others of their kind, on an island so near the main-land that a balsa could easily have reached it had the natives been disposed to venture. Fortunately for Pizarro, the Indians of that coast were not seafarers, and he was not molested. But if they had known how near to them and how defenceless existed that man who was to cause them and their kindred untold misery, by sending over a few balsa-loads of warriors they might have saved their kingdom from destruction.

V

SUCCESS IN SIGHT AT LAST

1528-1529

THE weary months went by without a sign of succor. Oppressed by famine, worn with watching for the sail that did not appear, the Spaniards would have welcomed any diversion, even an invasion by the Indians, rather than longer endure that life of inaction. Day by day, from earliest morn to night, they vainly scanned the heaving bosom of the Pacific, until at last they settled down into sullen despair. The promised land lay within their sight, the glittering spires and domes of the snow-crested Andes beckoned them mockingly ; but these famishing islanders had no means of sailing over to the main, save their clumsy raft, upon which they would be utterly defenceless.

They had resolved, at last, that death by slow starvation was to be their fate, believing themselves utterly abandoned, when, one day, a sail was sighted tossing on the waves. It drew near the island, but might have passed it had not Pizarro and his men rushed to a conspicuous headland and waved a banner, at the same time shooting off their arquebuses. It was a small craft to which that sail belonged, but it was found to be well stored with provisions and munitions, though with only just men enough aboard to navigate it. Sent by the faithful Almagro and Luque, who had used the last of their resources in outfitting it, even this small vessel had been allowed by the governor to sail only on condition that it should return within six months. Governor Rios had felt it incumbent upon him to rescue these reckless outcasts, even though they had disobeyed him by marooning themselves in the enemies' waters; but he imposed upon them the necessity of returning within half a year, under penalty of imprisonment if they did not obey.

"We accept the conditions," cried Pizarro; and his men, refreshed by the food they had eaten, and fortified by the resolution of their commander, assented with a shout.

"The prison yawns for us, anyway, if we return," continued Pizarro, "for all of us are in debt, even for the swords we carry and the armor we wear. Then, on, say I; perchance we may win fame and fortune yet!"

"On, on!" shouted the gallant men. "To the limit of our time. On to Peru!"

So they sailed away from Gorgona; and it seemed as if Dame Fortune mocked them, for, when in this condition, with a scant dozen of faithful adherents and only a single ship provisioned for six months, Pizarro found the kingdom and the opportunity to take it he had sought so long!

Southward, ever southward, sailed this little company of the most determined navigators since the days of Columbus. They passed the southernmost point reached by Ruiz, the pilot, who was aboard, and ardently serving Pizarro; they crossed the equinoctial line, and, after sailing for weeks in waters never before entered by Spaniards, reached the Gulf of Guayaquil.

Twenty days after leaving Gorgona they landed at an island which Pizarro named Santa Clara, and here found many images of men and beasts made of gold and silver, curiously wrought. The island was a sacred spot, visited by the Indians at stated times, when they left here their offerings, consisting of the golden objects mentioned and richly colored mantles woven of native wool. The Spaniards greatly desired to appropriate these treasures, but they refrained; not because the spot in which they were found was held sacred, but on account of the danger in offending the natives. They were too weak to engage in pillage, declared Pizarro, and must consider this voyage one of exploration merely.

"But we will remember what we saw, and where we saw it," he added, significantly; "*for we shall return*, and then, my children, you will revel in wealth such as mortal man never had before!"

While sustaining his men with promises, however, and holding them back from snatching at the gold almost within their grasp, he could not refrain from bitterly reflecting upon the hard fortune which had placed him in the position of Tantalus. And after they had crossed the great bay, and saw upon its farther shore a city of temples and palaces, their snow-white walls rivalling the frozen dome of Chimborazo, and probably containing treasures of gold and silver, he gnashed his teeth with vexation and rage.

But when he saw the craggy fortress dominating all, the swarms of people pouring forth from streets and dwellings, and the warriors by thousands assembling, or embarking on board the balsas in the harbor, he shrugged his shoulders and thought upon the cacique's warning: not to attempt the reduction of Peru without at least a thousand soldiers.

So it was not as a soldier, but as a "man of peace," proclaiming good-will and good faith, that he approached this newly discovered town of Tumbez and asked permission to interview its governor. It was one of the Inca's subject cities, inhabited by *mitamies*, or conquered colonists, and ruled by a *curaca*, or tributary cacique, but it was wealthy and powerful. In response to Pizarro's intimation that some fresh provisions would be acceptable, the curaca sent a balsa to the vessel, laden with game, fish, and tropical fruits, besides a number of llamas – the first of these curious animals ever seen by Europeans. Rude drawings of them had been shown Pizarro when he and Balboa reached the Pacific, but these were the first he had looked upon in the flesh.

The balsa was in charge of a Peruvian noble, who was also the first man of rank the Spaniards had met, all they had seen hitherto having been of the teeming common class. He was a stately, dignified personage, and magnificently apparelled, but his ears were shockingly deformed by the insertion of huge ornaments of gold several inches in diameter. These glittering disks of gold were the most conspicuous things about him, and caused the Spaniards to nickname him the "*Orejon*" a word derived from the Spanish *oreja*, an ear.

As he was received by Pizarro with distinction, shown all over the ship, feasted and wined, he was greatly pleased, and on his departure invited his host to visit him ashore. On the morrow, Pizarro sent ashore one of his trusty cavaliers named Molina, with a negro servant bearing a present of swine and poultry for the governor. Not only was this Molina the first white man the inhabitants of Tumbez had seen on their native soil, but the negro, the swine, and the poultry were the first objects of their kind ever landed there. They crowded around by thousands, respectful and courteous, but filled with awe and admiration.

They knew not which to admire most, the fair complexion and flowing beard of the white man, or the kinky wool and sable skin of the negro. The latter, they thought, must be artificially colored, so they tried to rub off the coloring, greatly to the glee of the black man, who showed his teeth and rolled his eyes, which pleased the Indians mightily. They were further entertained when one of the cocks crowed lustily, and wanted to know what that strange bird was saying. Molina was hospitably received at the curaca's palace, served with food and drink from gold and silver vessels, and finally departed greatly impressed with the wealth and magnificence of the Inca's palace. His tales seemed so wild and extravagant that Pizarro (deeming it unwise to leave the vessel and go ashore himself) sent that gallant knight Pedro de Candia in his stead. He had a fine figure, and being clad entirely in steel armor, with helmet and cuirass, a shining sword in his right hand and an arquebuse over his shoulder, the simple Indians were dazzled by his appearance. He appeared to them a veritable "child of the sun," indeed, and when, at their request, he caused his arquebuse to "speak to them" – when they heard the stunning report, and saw the flash, the smoke, and the destruction wrought by the ball it sent forth – they fell to the ground as if ready to worship him. Especially pleased with this handsome cavalier were the "brides of the Inca," or Virgins of the Sun, who, though immured within great walls of masonry, yet managed to gain a glimpse of him as he wandered through the convent gardens set with flowers and fruits in gold and silver.

The report carried by Candia to his commander made Pizarro "mad with joy," while at the same time he was deeply chagrined that he could not land and consummate his discovery by conquest. Being on his "good behavior," however, and unable to plunder those golden gardens, those temples sheathed with silver plates, those palaces furnished with vessels of gold, he reluctantly sailed on his course again, but resolved that no portion of that rich treasure should escape him. This voyage was the result of years of effort, the realization of hopes deferred, of schemes delayed ; and having waited so long, he could afford to contain himself yet a while longer. So Pizarro reasoned, for he was a philosopher, perhaps a fatalist, believing that whatever happened must be accepted for what it was worth – at all events, accepted.

That he amply rewarded himself for his restraint on this voyage, when he did not dare to plunder, much less massacre, and bore himself with an air of benignity which captivated the hearts of the natives, will appear in some of the succeeding chapters. It will then be seen that his benevolence was but a mask behind which he hid his true character, which displays a ferocity equalled by that of few men mentioned in the annals of America.

The voyage was continued to a point nine degrees south of the line, where, off the mouth of the Santa River, a broad stream flowing through an arid country, he turned about for Panama. Nothing was to be gained by going on, and scant time remained for regaining Panama within the prescribed period. He felt no misgivings now, to be sure, for he had proved his contention as to the existence of a kingdom, an empire – or at least a rich and wonderful country – abounding in natural wealth and teeming with half-civilized people.

So, northward the vessel's prow was turned, and homeward the happy voyagers set themselves, stopping on the way at a port named by Pizarro Santa Cruz, where they were entertained by a native princess. Their reception here reminds one of that given Don Bartholomew Columbus by the Haitian princess, Anacaona, for the Spaniards were met by dancing throngs of maidens, chanting to the music of primitive instruments, and a bountiful feast was prepared and served in arbors thatched with fragrant grasses.

The native character of the aborigines in America, whether of the West Indies or Peru, was very similar throughout, and though the latter were cast in sterner mould than the islanders, they showed themselves susceptible to kindness and fair treatment. If only the character in which Pizarro and his companion Spaniards appeared to the natives had been real, and not assumed; if their benevolence had been innate, and not a sham, the Indians might have been won over, and the conquest of Peru achieved without the bloodshed with which it was stained.

Such confidence had Pizarro in these people, that, touching in at Tumbez, on the homeward voyage, he allowed two or three of his men to remain there, taking with him in exchange two Indian youths, whom he afterwards made great use of as interpreters. One of them, in fact, who was called Felipillo, served him throughout his next campaign in this capacity, and exerted, by false interpretation, a malign influence upon the fate of Inca Atahuallpa.

A direct course was shaped from Tumbez to Panama, with a brief tarry only at Gorgona, to take aboard two sick Spaniards who had been left there in care of some friendly Indians. One alone survived, and after he had been rescued, the voyage was resumed. Good weather attended all the way to Panama, at which port the little band of heroes arrived in safety, after some of them, including their intrepid leader, had been absent eighteen months.

Pizarro and his partners were now courted and fawned upon, for at last they had achieved success, at last their persistence had received its reward. But, though they had proved the existence of the country which all along the Panamans had declared was wholly mythical; though Pizarro exhibited the strange animals, the llamas, and the cloths woven from their wool; though he dazzled the eyes of the commonalty with the gems and gold he had obtained by barter, the governor was yet obdurate. He might as well have been old Pedrarias himself, so far as granting favors to the trio was concerned. While he was not vicious, nor crafty, he was cautious and incredulous, declaring that lives enough had been sacrificed already" by the cheap display of gold and silver toys and a few Indian sheep."

This was the truth, and was intended as a rebuke to Pizarro and his friends; but, unpalatable as it was to them, they resolved to make the most of that display until their object should have been accomplished. They had made three expeditions; but, while each one had penetrated farther than the one preceding, discovering something of importance until that time unknown, the diffusion of knowledge was not the object they had aimed at. For that alone they cared nothing; they desired to be recompensed for their outlay. As the governor would not consent to another venture, much less aid in it, they resolved, in conference, to appeal to a higher authority – in fact, to lay their cause before the King of Spain.

After a vast deal of discussion, during which the old jealousies flamed up anew between Almagro and Pizarro, at last it was determined that the latter should go to Spain with their project. Almagro could not go, for he himself realized that his very appearance would turn the face of royalty away from the scheme; the clerigo could not go because of his duties; thus it remained to Pizarro, who, all finally agreed, was the man for the venture. He had been the principal actor in the events that made up the substance of their presentment; he was, moreover, despite his lack of education and his many years in the forests, courtly and dignified. He had inherited from his father, old Gonzalo, the cavalier, that inborn dignity which is the peculiar attribute of the Spanish hidalgo. He was ignorant of letters, it is true, but in a rude way he was eloquent, and his confidence in himself was such that no court, king, or queen, could bring him to confusion.

So he was sent on the mission to Spain, Almagro and Luque assenting thereto; but the latter expressing his distrust of Pizarro, nevertheless, in a "left-handed compliment" at parting. "Please God," he is said to have remarked, "that you do not steal the blessing, one from the other, as Jacob did from Esau; but I would that you had gone together!" This was a pretty plain intimation to Pizarro that he had better walk in the straight and narrow path, and to Almagro that he might become the victim of a misplaced confidence.

VI

AN APPEAL TO THE CROWN

1528-1530

ACCOMPANIED by Pedro de Candia as a companion, and several Indians as captives, Pizarro embarked for Spain in the early part of 1528. Besides the Indians, as specimens of the new country's products, he took with him a pair of llamas, or Peruvian sheep, many colored fabrics woven from their wool, and a rich collection of barbaric ornaments in gold and silver. He imitated his kinsman, Cortés, in respect to presenting himself before the court with gifts to please the king; for these astute conquerors knew the weakness of the royal Charles, whose appetite for gold was as insatiable as their own.

The resident partners at Panama had, by great exertion, and only after straining their credit to the utmost, raised the sum of fifteen hundred ducats, which they gave Pizarro, with an injunction to make the most of it, as no more would be forthcoming. He came near losing the whole of it, however, soon after landing in Spain, for that wary individual, Lawyer Enciso, who had been with Pizarro and Balboa at Darien, brought out an ancient claim for debts, and clapped the would-be conqueror into jail.

This was the reception offered Pizarro when, for the first time in twenty years, he returned to his native land. His great services to the crown were forgotten, and the only man who remembered him, it seemed, was the rascally lawyer, Enciso. No, there was one other – the king. Charles had been informed of his coming, and thinking there might be somewhat of profit in an expedition which he was called upon to sanction merely – that is, give permission for the invasion of a country not his own, and the plundering of a people over whom he did not rule – he ordered Pizarro to be released. Not alone that, but he ordered him to appear before him at court, then being held at Toledo.

Pizarro was not slow in complying with the royal mandate, and was delighted, when he arrived at court, to find there his distant relative, Cortés, who had come for redress of grievances. The two made common cause, it is said, or, at all events, Cortés coached his uncouth cousin in the etiquette of the court, and even spoke a good word for him to the king. There is "honor among thieves," according to the ancient maxim, and when a number of rascals get together for the purpose of plundering honest and peace-loving citizens, they are usually true to one another –

until after the plundering has been effected. This trio of plunderers, Charles, Cortés, and Pizarro, laid their heads together, as it were, and perfected a scheme for the pillaging of Peru.

King Charles was in a hurry to get away from Spain, having a foreign war on his hands; but he was never averse to engaging in any venture that promised him funds with which to conduct his wars, so, before he left, he recommended Pizarro to the Council of the Indies, and requested his consort to expedite the matter all she could. It was the custom with the court of Castile, however, to "make haste slowly," and a year passed before the Empress finally executed a "capitulation," by which Pizarro was authorized to proceed with his scheme. This capitulation may have been prepared by the orders of Charles's queen, but was actually in the name of his unfortunate mother, *Juana Loca*, or, as the Spaniards called her, "Crazy Jane." So, after all, two women, and one of them a lunatic, had more to do with the project than the vagrant ruler of Spain.

However, the contract was finally drawn up and signed, by which Pizarro was empowered to raise, mainly at his own expense, a force of two hundred and fifty men, one hundred of whom might come from the colonies, and embark them in three vessels for the isthmus. In return for what he had done, and what he was to do – namely, effect the conquest of Peru and divert its vast wealth into the coffers of Castile, assist at the conversion of its inhabitants and promote the "cause of religion "as understood by the Spaniards – he was to be made governor and captain-general, also adelantado and alguacil mayor of the conquered province – when it was conquered. He was to receive a salary of seven hundred and twenty-five thousand *maravedis* after he had found the funds with which to pay it; was to be allowed a repartimiento of Indians – after he had captured them; was made a knight of Santiago, and privileged to quarter the royal arms with those of the Pizarros on his family shield. Somebody was unkind enough to insinuate that a "hog couchant" was the proper design for one who, according to rumor, had been suckled by a sow; but, in fact, Pizarro was allowed to adopt an "Indian city, with a vessel in the distance on the waters, and the llama of Peru."

A modest legend recited that "Under the auspices of Charles, and by the industry, the resources, and the genius of Pizarro, this country was discovered and conquered." This motto may have been considered premature; but even so, it was prophetic. To undertake was to accomplish, with Pizarro. He regarded the country as good as conquered, and as at no time had he wavered in his faith, so he was honest in his endeavors to inspire his followers with his sentiments.

These adventurers were not so many as he desired to raise, and even when he paid a visit to his native Truxillo, though his friends and kinsmen were agape at his elevated state, having in mind his departure from that place years before, a fugitive swineherd, very few enlisted beneath his banner. His father, the reprobate Gonzalo, had been dead many years, also his mother; but he found four brothers, who were proud to claim relationship with him, and who, being poor, were glad to embrace the opportunity he offered them for becoming rich. Only one of them, Hernando, was the legitimate son of old Gonzalo – as he frequently reminded his brothers – while of the others: Juan, Gonzalo, and Martin Alcantara, only the last-named owned the same mother as Francisco.

As they were without binding family ties, and blessed with few possessions save their inordinate pride, the four brothers lost little time in joining their distinguished relative at Seville. When he arrived there from Truxillo, Francisco found, to his mortification, that the full complement of men had not been raised, and that, the six months in which he had promised to be ready for the voyage having expired, the Council of the Indies might prevent him from sailing. The condition of his ships was not what it should have been, either, and so, in order to evade an official investigation, he set sail in a hurry, one night in January, 1530, from the port of San Lucar.

Hernando followed after with two ships, and, joining him at Gomera in the Canaries, together they crossed the ocean without mishap.

Landing at Nombre de Dios, on the northern coast of the isthmus, opposite Panama, Pizarro was met by Luque and Almagro, who had waited impatiently for tidings from Spain, and could not restrain themselves any longer. What they learned was not to their satisfaction, as may be imagined, for, while the priest had been raised to the bishopric of Tumbez, and made "protector of the Peruvian Indians," Almagro was to be commandant of the Tumbez fortress only, with a salary of three hundred thousand maravedis. He was, to be sure, raised to the rank of an hidalgo; but that, despite his lowly condition, he spurned as an empty honor. He declared that Pizarro had appropriated all the honors and emoluments of the projected conquest, and said sarcastically that he wondered why he had not had himself "appointed a bishop, as well as governor-general, adelantado, etc., etc."

It had been agreed between them, in advance, that Almagro should at least receive the position of adelantado, or lieutenant-governor; while Ruiz, the pilot, was to be made alguacil mayor. Instead, however, Pizarro came back with all the honors thickly clustered around his own head, and that is what the trio received in return for their trust in him.

Ruiz was to be "Grand Pilot of the Southern Sea," but that was because Pizarro was not a seafaring man; Pedro de Candia was made master of artillery, but, as all men knew, Pizarro could not fire a cannon; and the clerigo was created a bishop, for the sole reason that Pizarro had not taken holy orders! In this strain ran on Almagro, working himself into a passion, which was not allayed by the sight of the four brothers of Pizarro standing about, their faces wreathed in sardonic smiles. Hernando especially, the only legitimate Pizarro of the group, made himself particularly obnoxious to the small but valiant Almagro, his contempt for whom he took no pains to conceal. From that interview at Nombre de Dios dates the feud between these two soldiers, which ended only when the ill-fated Almagro lost his head.

Pizarro, of course, protested that he had done his best to secure the coveted honors for Almagro, but, in sooth, the Emperor was determined he himself should have them all. It was not so much that he considered him the more worthy of the two, but, as a matter of policy, he had decreed that the highest offices should be vested in a single individual, in order that he alone should be responsible! However, it did not matter, of course, for, as Almagro knew full well, whatever his partner owned he would share with him, even to the whole of his wealth and his titular honors. He would resign the adelantadoship – he would, indeed – and induce the Emperor to confer it upon his "most faithful friend" Almagro.

This he swore, by the Virgin, and "*por Dios*" and by all the saints in the calendar; and he swore glibly, too, until happening to glance up he caught the eye of the clerigo fixed upon him. Then he halted, stammered, and the semblance of a blush stole over his bronzed cheek; for the clerigo was smiling grimly, incredulously, and he recalled his remark when they had parted two years before: "God grant that one of you may not defraud the other of his share!"

Fully convinced that Pizarro intended to bestow such lucrative positions as he himself did not hold upon his brothers, and that henceforth there was no hope for his own advancement, while the partnership continued, Almagro loudly proclaimed his disgust, and announced his intention of setting out on an expedition of his own. He was only dissuaded by Luque and the lawyer, Espinosa, both of whom were financially interested in the venture, and who, foreseeing the ruin of the enterprise unless Almagro should be placated, managed to patch up a truce between the principals.

Mollified by the promise of the adelantadoship as soon as it could be conveniently transferred,

Almagro embarked in the enterprise again with heart and soul; but there was thenceforth a feeling of distrust between the partners, even greater than had hitherto existed. It was mutually agreed that the Pizarro brothers should not be advanced at Almagro 's expense, and that the original articles of the compact should be carried out. Indeed, had not the blessing of God been called down upon it, and, in a manner equally solemn, His curses invoked upon whoever should break it?

After the cargoes of the three ships had been transferred across the isthmus, and the soldiers marched over that rugged pathway between Nombre de Dios and Panama, three new vessels were purchased and equipped. The difficulties of this transfer, which included all the armament of the ships, as well as passengers and cargo, were stupendous. Few, if any, beasts of burden were available at that distant day; there were no wheeled vehicles of transport, and no roads worthy the name, only trails and Indian foot-paths through the mountains. To add to the troubles of the trio, many of their men deserted, alarmed at the reports received on the isthmus, of cannibal natives awaiting them in Peru, escaping which they would surely die of famine or fevers. Thus many of the weaklings were weeded out; but in the end the three vessels sailed from Panama well laden, carrying one hundred and eighty men, among them nearly thirty cavalry. They were the pick of Spain, as well as of Panama, and as for the armament, it was the most complete Pizarro had ever obtained. It was not, as a whole, equal to what had been stipulated in the contract with the crown; but there was no interference from royal officials, and the fleet was allowed to proceed.

First, however, as on a former occasion, the entire command assembled in the cathedral of Panama, where the clerigo and other *reverendos*, who had been sent out to convert the heathen, invoked the blessing of the Most High upon the banners of Pizarro. Then the holy edifice echoed to roll of drum and blare of trumpet, as, led by the Governor, Pizarro, Luque, and Almagro, the mailed soldiers marched forth into the street, where they were greeted by loud huzzas from the people. A second time Pizarro was escorted to his ships by the entire populace of Panama; and as by this time the man's constancy and determination had won all hearts, he departed amid wild enthusiasm.

It is easy to cheer on the leader of a forlorn hope, and urge him to continue to the end; but taking active part in the affair is quite a different matter. Few of the residents were inclined to go with Pizarro, their memories running back to the sufferings endured by him and his companions on other occasions. They had been rewarded, to be sure – those who had survived – most of them with promises; but those who clung to Pizarro on the island – the "immortal twelve" – had been created hidalgos. They were now the "sons of somebody," these men, most of whom were, in fact, the sons of nobody in particular, and were looked up to as "Dons," of high degree. The airs they assumed were almost insufferable; but, their rewards having been won by merit, their pretensions were good-naturedly tolerated. But not so those of the four brothers of Pizarro, who incurred the enmity of many besides the fiery old Almagro, by their display of pride and arrogance. Shaking his sword at their retreating forms, as they were rowed off to the ship, he growled in the ear of the clerigo: "The beggarly bastards think themselves soldiers, because, forsooth, they for the first time in their lives have put on casque and corselet. Por Dios! I wish they had but one throat to the four, and I had my grip upon it."

"Nay, nay, amigo," returned the clerigo, "curse them not. It is but natural that Francisco should desire his brothers with him. And, remember our compact; perchance he may keep it!"

"Ay, perchance," grumbled Almagro; "but not if that ill-favored Hernando has his will. It is he I fear - nay, not fear, but distrust. As for any love he and his misbegotten brothers bear Francisco –

why, he never heard of them until he had returned to Truxillo, I trow. And he prefers them to his friend Almagro."

"Well, we have done our part, my friend; if Francisco doeth not his, we may leave him to be dealt with by God. The stakes are large and well worth playing for. There, see, they hoist their sails. Now they are off; there goes a gun, and another –"

"Faith, they'd better save their powder," interrupted Almagro. "Think of the trouble we had to get it! Sulphur and charcoal, and all that, are not to be had for the asking, as you know."

"Yes, I know," sighed the clerigo. "For years, now, we've been toiling, as you say, saving and spending, in order that Francisco may achieve that conquest over the heathen; and now –"

"Now he's off, and Panama will never see him again! But," added Almagro, fiercely, "I shall soon follow after! He will be sending back, as usual, for soldiers and horses, powder and arquebuses; but will he get them? Nay, for the next command goes out under Don Diego de Almagro, comandante of Tumbez, and adelantado in prospect of Peru!"

VII

ON THE PERUVIAN FRONTIER

1531-1532

ON a day in January, 1531, nearly three years after his departure for Spain, Pizarro launched the fourth and largest expedition, for which he had been so long preparing, and in which he had invested everything he possessed. His ships were freighted with his hopes, as well, for he never despaired of achieving the conquest upon which he had set his heart.

Having in mind the treasures he had seen at Tumbez, and doubting not they were yet awaiting him, he issued orders for his pilots to steer straight for the gulf of Guayaquil, upon which that port was situated. Baffling winds and currents forced him to land at a point about sixty miles from Tumbez; but still, despite these obstacles, he traversed in fourteen days a distance it had taken him two years to gain in his previous attempts.

Landing his troops in the province of Coaque, Pizarro marched them along the shore, while the ships pursued a parallel course by sea, and in this manner he approached and surprised an Indian village. The inhabitants came forth to greet him amicably, as they had done before, relying upon the supposed friendliness of the strangers; but, having arrived in strength and with power, the Spaniards cast off the cloak of humanity, which they had assumed in their weakness, and fell upon the Indians like fiends. They fled in terror as the soldiers, sword in hand, ravaged the village of all they possessed, not only of gold, silver, and gems, but of food as well. A vast amount of spoil was obtained, which, boasted Pizarro, would never have been found if they had not surprised the natives before they could secrete it.

"Hereafter, comrades," he said, as he harangued his men in the deserted village, "we will do as we have done to-day. The friendship of the natives is a good thing, but their treasure is what we are after. We will pursue this course at Tumbez, for there we shall find enough to enrich us all. This is but paltry plunder to what we shall find at Tumbez!"

Still, there was gold, in ornaments and grains; and as for emeralds, they were so numerous that the Spaniards did not realize their value. Some were found as large as birds' eggs; but the best of them were destroyed by the soldiers, on the advice of one Fray Reginaldo, a Dominican monk, who had come out to convert the heathen, but who was not averse to despoiling them of their riches. Fray Reginaldo advised the soldiers to test the stones with a hammer. If they broke, they were not precious stones, but if they did not break they were true emeralds, said Fray Reginaldo. The simple soldiers took his advice, and thus lost their gems; but it was noticed that the monk did not submit his own emeralds (of which he had a goodly number secreted about his person) to this rude test. On the contrary, he preserved them all intact, and on his return to Panama disposed of them at values greatly enhanced by the destruction of the soldiers' emeralds, which, if they had been saved and sold, might have caused a glut in the market.

No soldier was allowed to plunder for himself, solely, but was obliged, under pain of death, to make a return to his commander of everything he had taken. The pillage of this Indian village was brought together in a heap, and after deducting the "royal fifth" – or the amount that was always reserved for the crown – the remainder was divided among the soldiers in proportion to their rank. Pizarro dealt more fairly by his men, when dividing the spoils, than Cortés in Mexico, and they rarely had occasion to complain. Realizing the necessity existing for making an impression upon the people of Panama, he concluded to send the bulk of this pillage back to the isthmus, together with the vessels comprising his small squadron. It amounted to twenty thousand *castellanos*, or more than two hundred thousand dollars, and when it reached Panama created a great sensation.

The effect upon the Panamans was what Pizarro had calculated, and reinforcements were sent back by the returning ships; but, unfortunately, the resources of the isthmus in respect to population were not too great. Still, there is little doubt that Pizarro never could have accomplished anything in Peru, had it not been .for that convenient way-station established by old Pedrarias on the south coast of the isthmus. Panama and Pizarro are of necessity linked together in the conquest of Peru, and, poor as was the support afforded the conqueror by the infant settlement, he could not have existed without it.

After several months of marching and waiting, during which the little army suffered terribly from an epidemic that laid many a soldier low, a vessel arrived off the coast containing provisions. It also brought as passengers the royal officials, such as the *veedor*, or inspector, king's treasurer, and comptroller, who had been left behind in the haste of departure from Spain, and whose presence was not over-welcome, as they were not soldiers, but spies. A more acceptable addition to Pizarro's force was that of a valiant officer named Benalcazar, who joined him with thirty soldiers. These about supplied the places of those lost by disease, and Pizarro continued his march along the shores of Guayaquil until he arrived opposite the island of Puná. He was then on the mainland, and had no craft of any kind in which to reach the island, where he purposed to establish a camp and await the arrival of reinforcements.

This island lies at the mouth of the Guayaquil river, is about twenty miles in length by four in breadth, and at the time of Pizarro's visit was covered with magnificent forests. While he was pondering upon the problem of how to reach it without boats, the cacique of the island chanced to come over to the main-land with a number of attendants. He not only cordially invited Pizarro to visit him, but offered to ferry his army across on balsas, which, without delay, his men constructed on the spot, of materials obtained in the forest. They were so large and so buoyant, that the whole army went over on them together with the guns, baggage, and horses.

A camp was pitched in a beautiful grove on a headland, whence a view was afforded of the bay, and distant Tumbez across the waters, and where the Spaniards were daily visited by thousands of Indians, who professed the greatest joy at being allowed to entertain them as guests. Their manifestations of gladness were so extravagant that Pizarro finally became suspicious, and, sending spies into the forest and fields, discovered that his professed friends were drilling their warriors for battle and making weapons for warfare, such as arrows, bows, spears, and javelins. They had drawn Pizarro into a trap, and were about to spring it; but the grim soldier was not one to await the movements of an enemy. His motto was ever, "Well begun, half won," and to begin well meant, with him, a sharp and sudden attack before the enemy was aware of his designs. A number of chiefs had met in a hut to consult together upon the best means for destroying their enemy. Informed of this by his interpreter, Pizarro surrounded the hut with his soldiers, and captured every one. The chiefs protested their innocence, but their enemies, the Indians of Tumbez, some of whom had come over to greet the Spaniards, declared they were worthy of death, so they were permitted by Pizarro to kill them. They beheaded these unfortunate caciques, every one, and the result was that their people rose in insurrection, whether they had intended earlier to do so or not. The little band of Spaniards, less than two hundred in number, was soon surrounded by thousands of savages, whooping, howling, and fighting with demoniac fury. Amid showers of darts and arrows, Pizarro and his brothers led a charge upon the Indians, in which a few of the Spaniards fell to rise no more, and Hernando Pizarro was wounded by a javelin in the leg.

The savages, however, were repulsed, and fled in terror to the deeper forest, whence, for days afterwards, they emerged singly or in small parties, for the purpose of cutting off stragglers and sentinels. This mode of warfare the Spaniards could not successfully combat, and it was becoming excessively annoying, when they were greatly relieved, one day, by the sight of a vessel approaching the island. It was filled with volunteers, to the number of one hundred or more, under the command of Fernando de Soto. This opportune arrival of the cavalier who subsequently discovered the Mississippi, bringing with him the veterans of Nicaragua, as well as spare horses for the cavalry, put a different face on the affair. Pizarro now had at his command a well-equipped force of about three hundred men, and felt strong enough to carry out his designs against the city of Tumbez. Embarking his soldiers in the ship, therefore, and lading the horses and baggage upon balsas, he crossed the gulf to the main-land. He anticipated some resistance from the inhabitants of Tumbez, as at the time of his first visit it was strongly fortified and filled with warriors; but he was not prepared for what he did experience, when, having landed on the main-land, he formed his forces for the attack. In the first place, the natives cut off one of his balsas by stratagem and killed three of his men; in the second, when he advanced with his soldiers, to storm the city if it resisted, or to treat with its people if they were inclined to surrender, he found it entirely deserted. During the long interval between his arrival at Puná and his descent upon Tumbez, the inhabitants of the latter place had received correct information as to the real intentions of the Spaniards. They knew, at last, the character of the men who, only a few years before, had come in the guise of peaceful missionaries, who spurned their gifts of gold, and who affected heart-felt concern as to their souls' salvation.

The Indians of Coaque had sent word of their rapine, those of Puná, could testify as to their lust for blood, and the dwellers in Tumbez concluded to retreat before it was too late. They not only deserted their city, but so far as they could demolished it, so that only the fortress and the great temple remained intact, though stripped of their golden decorations. The priests and nobles had fled, taking with them all their treasures; the "brides of the Inca" also had disappeared, taking with them the rare flowers of gold and silver that had bloomed in their gardens; while of the two Spaniards who had been left here by Pizarro, there was not the slightest trace.

Then, perhaps, Pizarro doubted the wisdom of his policy of rapine – when his soldiers, bereft of the last hope of sharing the treasures they were told Tumbez contained, murmured and muttered, almost rebelled. Promises were no longer of avail to pacify, neither would threats subdue them, so Pizarro placed himself at their head and led them into the country. The curaca of Tumbez was captured, but no satisfaction was obtained from him, though through his efforts a scroll of paper was delivered by an Indian to Pizarro, on which had been written, by one of the Spaniards left in his charge on the first visit: "Know ye, whoever ye may be that may chance to set foot in this country, that it contains more gold and silver than there is iron in Biscay!" Whether, as the disappointed soldiers insinuated, this paper was a mere device of their commander to keep alive their expectations, or whether it was really genuine, the truth of its statement was made manifest ere many months had passed. The land of the Incas was a land of gold, indeed, only the surface deposits of which had been gathered by the Peruvians, and many a galleon was to sail from the isthmus to Spain, laden with a golden cargo.

Sending out De Soto and his cavalry to reconnoitre in the foot-hills, Pizarro advanced with the main army along the coast. He had convinced himself, at last, that the policy of pillage was not the true one, for he found that it angered the people and that news of his doings was transmitted ahead of him, to his great disadvantage. So he ordered that the natives, when met with, should be unmolested, unless they themselves provoked an attack. This meant that few deeds of violence were done at that time, as the natives were responsive to good treatment and rarely, if ever, began hostilities. On the contrary, they received the invaders with hospitality, feeding them from their scanty stock of supplies, and providing them with shelters at night.

So Pizarro again assumed the role of missionary, proclaiming peace and good-will, as before. His reason for this appears, when we reflect that he had now cut loose from his base of supplies on the coast, and was advancing into unknown country. What was before him he knew not, but, from scattered fragments of information obtained through his interpreters, he learned that the ruler of the land was not so very far away, and probably awaiting his coming, with countless thousands of trained warriors. It would not be good policy, therefore, to leave a hostile population between his army and the coast, which in case of his defeat might rise and massacre. More than a year had elapsed since his departure from Panama, for he left Tumbez early in May, 1532, and a month later might have been found in the beautiful valley of the Piura, the fertility of which, proclaimed by verdant fields and most luxuriant vegetation, induced him to halt and found a city. A site was selected, and with extraordinary diligence the soldiers worked at the quarrying of stone, cutting of timber, and erection of buildings, with such success that soon this first European colony in Peru could boast a fortress, a city hall, a church, and a king's store-house, besides other structures of lesser importance.

They did not labor unassisted, for the Indians were forced to contribute their services. In fact, they probably performed the greater part of the labor, as, soon after the organization of a municipal government, they were apportioned among the colonists, together with the rich lands in the vicinity. Thus that pernicious system of slavery, known as repartimientos, was established in Peru, as it had already been for years in the West Indies and Mexico. Even the monks who accompanied Pizarro as missionaries were in favor of this arrangement, as (in the words of one who was intimate with the commander), "It being evident that the colonists could not support themselves without the services of the Indians, the religious instructors and our leaders all agreed that it would serve the cause of religion, and tend greatly to their spiritual welfare, since they would thus have the opportunity of being initiated in the true faith, conforming to the mandates of his majesty!"

Thus the new city was founded, and the people to whom the land belonged on which it stood were enslaved, in the name of religion and the cross! The audacity of its founders was only equalled by their hypocrisy; but both these qualities served them well in the coming crisis of their lives.

VIII

A GLANCE AT THE PERUVIANS

IN order to understand the nature of this enterprise projected by Pizarro – to grasp its magnitude, and fully comprehend its perils, we should pause a while – before proceeding with him into the unknown country, and inform ourselves as to its resources. How did it differ from any other portion of South America, and why was this territory better worth invading than any other?

In the first place, it was unique in its geographical situation, physical conditions, and natural resources. It seemed as though nature had outdone herself in creating the stupendous Andes, with peaks rising more than twenty thousand feet into the clouds, and stored with an inexhaustible supply of precious metals. A continuous mountain chain, or *cordillera*, ran almost parallel with the trend of the coast, between which and this "backbone of the continent" exists every variety of table-land, or elevated plain, fertile valley, gloomy gorge, ravine, and arid desert country.

The ancient empire of the Incas, which Pizarro had so audaciously invaded, was comprehended within the present limits of Peru, and overlapped its northern boundaries. It extended from two or three degrees north of the equator to thirty-seven or thirty-eight south of it, and from the Pacific on the west to the headwaters of the Amazon on the east. Perhaps we might better say that its boundaries, except on the Pacific, were indeterminate, since no obstacle of a physical nature seemed sufficient to deter the warlike Incas in their territorial conquests.

In the second place, this wonderful region, with every variety of climate from torrid to frigid, was occupied by an equally wonderful people, who, during the lapse of centuries had developed a civilization, state or condition of refinement, unequalled by that of any other aboriginal nation on the American continent. The Aztecs of Mexico in some respects surpassed these "Incas" of Peru – or, rather, they adopted and adapted the civilization of former peoples, as the Toltecs, and the Mayas of Yucatan, with their hieroglyphics and un surpassed architecture – but they were not, upon the whole, so advanced.

But for their thought-carrying "picture-writings" and their astronomical system (both, probably, inherited from the Toltecs), the Aztecs might be classed second to the Incas in civilization. The truth is, that each nation had advanced along special lines, the one excelling the other in some things; but in general culture the Peruvians probably surpassed the Mexicans. Each nation had developed in absolute ignorance of the other, separated as were these two peoples by Central America and the isthmian region; but if they had been conjoined, they might have risen to a plane hardly inferior to that occupied by some of the Old-World monarchies.

Had there been any sort of communication between the two during the years in which the conquest of Mexico and the West Indies was being achieved, the fate of Peru might have been different from what it was as history informs us. Not a hint, however, reached the Peruvians of what was going on outside their mountainous domain, save that vague rumor now and then disturbed them with the tidings of strangers in armor and with wonderful weapons, landing on the isthmus and flitting along their coast.

Within their limitations the Peruvians had evolved a most admirable system of government – more admirable, in fact, than that which the Spaniards imposed in its place. They had made great advances in agriculture, for not only had they cultivated the fertile valleys and plains, but they had terraced the sides of hills and mountains, and vivified the waste and desert places by conducting to them the waters of springs and mountain streams through aqueducts, some of which were hundreds of miles in length. They were also, strange to say, the only aborigines of America who were found in possession of domestic animals utilized as beasts of burden; for, as we know, there were no horses or cattle native to this country within the historic period. The nearest approach to them were the llamas, or "American camels," which, however, the Peruvians valued more for their fleece than as means of transport. Then there were the alpacas and vicunas, which existed in a wild state in the mountains and snowy regions, and were only gathered together at stated intervals by great hunts, in which fifty or sixty thousand men took part. But the llamas were domesticated, and from their fleece, and that of the alpacas and vicunas, were woven cloths of finest texture, which were dyed in beautiful and permanent colors.

The status of a people is generally judged by their architecture, and herein the Peruvians did not fall short of the standard; for, while the dwellings of the masses were humble huts of clay or straw, perhaps, those of the Inca and the nobles were massively constructed of stone. The country contained numerous temples and palaces which, though but a single story in height, were built of immense blocks of granite fitted together so nicely that the lines of junction could hardly be perceived. These vast masses of stone were sometimes quarried many leagues distant from the places in which the buildings were erected, and, working without the assistance of machinery – so far as known – the wonder is how the ancient Peruvians removed and placed them in position. The same wonder assails us when we contemplate the remains of their magnificent roads, with which the country was crossed. One of these is said to have been two thousand miles in length, and not only traversed vast stretches of valley and plain, but was carried over mountains and across ravines and gorges. The cities of Quito and Cuzco were thus united by a road three hundred leagues in length, twenty-five paces in breadth, enclosed within parapets, and watered at intervals by clear, running streams as well as shaded by odoriferous trees. It was composed of great blocks of freestone, accurately fitted together, and as smooth as glass on their upper surfaces.

When deep ravines were encountered they were filled with masonry, and streams that ran through gorges were crossed by means of hammock or suspension bridges, made of osiers woven into ropes and cables. Such bridges as these are in use to-day, and afford the only means of crossing those wild mountain streams, which flow at abysmal depths between almost perpendicular walls of rock.

Along the great stone highways, at intervals corresponding to a day's journey, comfortable stone houses were erected, supplied with every necessity for the traveller, and, being intended mainly for the army, containing not only provisions, such as maize and coca, but articles of clothing, arms, and martial equipments. And all these great works were performed by a people wholly unacquainted with the use of iron, whose tools were merely of stone, or of copper hardened by an admixture of tin. Gold and silver they had in abundance, but they did not make use of either as money – only for the purpose of ornamentation. The palaces of the Inca, and the temples, though severely massive as to their exteriors, without windows, arches, or columns, glittered inside with gold, and sometimes were ablaze with gems.

The ruler and his nobles ate with their fingers (which, as the old saying runs, were "made before forks"), but they were served from massive gold and silver plate; while the imagination of their artisans ran riot in producing unique forms of ewers, vases, bracelets, anklets, finger and ear rings, and other articles of personal adornment. Allusion has already been made to their skill in making artificial flowers of gold and silver, which exactly imitated the originals. They were also proficient in casting golden statues, some of them life-size, and in sculpture. In the mechanical arts, where patience and close attention were required, they greatly excelled; but their system of numeration was imperfect, and in astronomical lore they were deficient, though they possessed a rude calendar, spacing the year into twelve lunar months, and made solar observations with some degree of accuracy.

They possessed no written records, no picture-writings or hieroglyphic chronicles; but their place was supplied in a measure by the *quipu*, a contrivance "consisting of a main cord, from which hung at certain distances smaller cords of different colors, each having a special meaning, as silver, gold, corn, soldiers, etc. Single, double, and triple knots were tied in the smaller cords, representing definite numbers." This quipu, or cord, was "chiefly used for arithmetical purposes, and to register important facts or events"; but it served only to keep in mind the ideas with which each color or knot was associated. It thus assisted the memory of the chroniclers, who preserved the annals of the country by oral tradition, passed from one generation to another.

Was it not natural that, dwelling beneath or near the equator, the Peruvians should particularly honor the sun-god? They not only worshipped the sun, but they claimed that their first great ruler and his successors descended from that luminary. Myth and fable enshroud their origin, but their earliest tradition relates to this celestial origin, when the son and daughter of the orb of day, in the persons of Manco Capac and Mama Oello Huaco, came to earth, and founded the city of Cuzco. Thus Cuzco became their capital, and here was erected the glorious "Temple of the Sun," known also as the "Place of Gold," because of a great golden effigy of the sun, consisting of a central face of burnished gold with numerous blazing rays radiating to roof and walls and floor of the temple. It was of solid gold, but was also studded with gems, forming a beautiful and brilliant apparition of the deity from whom the Incas had descended.

Boasting this celestial origin, the *Inca Capac* (great or powerful lord) considered himself vastly superior to the common herd, and by his subjects was so regarded. He was their ruler, their master, in every sense, holding in his hands their lives, and literally their fortunes. In course of time the Inca became surrounded by a vast number of nobles, who could trace their origin to the original Capac through an innumerable company of concubines; but he was always supreme. Even the nobles could not approach the celestial presence, save with bowed and uncovered head, and bearing burdens on their shoulders, in token of submission and inferior station.

Being the high-priest of the people, as well as their monarch, all the temples and palaces were his, and these were numerous throughout all the land. They were, as already indicated, adorned with golden statues, cornices, and every variety of ornament, hung with gold-fringed

END WALL OF TEMPLE OF THE SUN, CUZCO

tapestries, and furnished with gem-studded plate of gold. While the Inca usually held aloof from the commonalty, he sometimes showed himself to his abject subjects, on which occasions they were dazzled by the display he made of gold and jewels.

The common people were not permitted to accumulate any sort of wealth whatever, all the gems and precious metals being reserved for the Inca. Even the lands they so assiduously cultivated were held by them only on sufferance, and while the laws of the country compelled every man and woman to marry at a certain age and set up a household by themselves, they owned neither home nor soil. Their lives were devoted to labor, but they accumulated nothing, though at the same time no person was permitted to want for the necessaries of life. The agriculturists tilled the soil, first for the Inca, then for the sun, finally for themselves, and the proceeds were apportioned accordingly. Likewise the artisans – the weavers of wool, the dyers, the gold and silver smiths, the potters, miners, masons – all worked for the enrichment of the state, which was, in effect, the

Inca.

The laws were few in number, but strictly enforced, and death was the penalty for theft, murder, blasphemy, arson, adultery, and rebellion. Human life lost its sacred character in a land ruled by a despot, who could slay at will and without question. But, while the Peruvians were scarcely more than mere human machines, made orderly and industrious by compulsion, they were carefully nurtured by the state, which made their welfare continually the object of its solicitude. The products of their lands and looms were carefully collected and stored in government warehouses, whence such as were needed were redistributed, the surplus being left for future demands. Thus it was that when the Spaniards reached Peru and penetrated the interior, they found vast supplies of grain, clothing, etc., accumulated by the provident and far-seeing government, under direction of the Inca and his nobles.

In one sense, the life led by the Peruvians was ideal, inasmuch as the people were removed from want, shielded in youth, and sheltered in old age; but it was not a life calculated to encourage ambition or personal effort, so that, while they had reached a certain stage of culture, there they remained fixed, like a vessel becalmed in a stagnant sea.

The common people, who composed the bulk of Peru's teeming population, did not need to think, for their thinking was done for them by the state. Yet the Inca and his nobles, who represented the brain and mind of this vast body politic, were not peculiarly fitted for directing the energies of the people. The mechanism had been formed for them centuries before, and they merely kept it in motion. When, as happened after the Spanish invasion, the hand and head that guided the machinery were removed, the whole system fell into confusion. The people were paralyzed by the capture of their Inca, for that was a mischance they had not contemplated, and before they had recovered, and ranged themselves under new leaders, the Spaniards had secured a hold which could not be shaken off. Thus the Peruvians defeated themselves, more surely than they were defeated by the Spaniards. Or, rather, they were crushed by their own system of government, which, when once its foundations were undermined, fell with a crash, involving both the nobility and the commonalty in universal ruin.

One of the most energetic of the Incas flourished towards the end of the fifteenth century. His name was Yupanqui, and he extended the territory of Peru from near the present borders of Chili to the southern boundary of Ecuador. He was assisted by his son, Huayna Capac, who, at the death of his father, which occurred in the last decade of that century which witnessed the discovery of America by Columbus, carried his conquests far beyond Quito. This city was the most important of the many conquests made by the Peruvians, and rivalled in its attractions Cuzco, the capital, with which the conqueror connected it by one of those wonderful roads, already mentioned.

After a long and successful reign, during which he extended to the utmost the limits of his kingdom, and perfected many of the great works commenced by former rulers, Huayna Capac died, and his embalmed body was borne to Cuzco, where it was deposited in the Temple of the Sun. In that magnificent pantheon, where the darkness was dispelled by the refulgent rays of the great, golden sun, typical of their celestial ancestry, all the Incas who had ever reigned were ranged against the walls. Their desiccated bodies were clothed in royal robes, and seated in chairs of gold, with bowed heads and hands crossed on their breasts. Some of them had sat there for centuries, except that on the occasion of certain religious festivals they were brought out into the light of day and entertained at ghastly banquets.

The body of Huayna Capac was taken to Cuzco, but his heart was retained in Quito, which in his latter years was his favorite place of residence. There had lived, also, his favorite wife, daughter of the last king of Quito, whom he had conquered and dethroned. By her he had a son, whom he named Atahuallpa, a word derived, it is said, from *Atahua*, valor, and *allpa*, meaning sweet. He loved Atahuallpa, who went with him on his campaigns, and was bright, fearless, and handsome. His mother had been a princess of Quito, and when on his death-bed, the Inca thought to make reparation for depriving her father of his throne, by making her son ruler over the northern portion of the kingdom.

But he had another son, who alone was the rightful heir to the crown, and whose mother was not only the Inca's wife, but his sister! This was in accordance with the immutable law of the Incas, repulsive as it may seem; and, though Huayna Capac had a multitude of lesser wives in his harem, the number of whose children was legion, he had but one legal wife, his sister, and left but one lawful heir to the throne at his death. This was Huascar Inca, then residing in Cuzco, and about thirty years old.

In the eyes of the law, then, Atahuallpa was illegitimate; but to him, at his father's death, was left the kingdom of Quito, while to Huascar remained the greater portion of the empire. Still, it was then a divided empire, and though for a few years the brothers continued in amicable relations, after a while Atahuallpa, the younger, became aggressive and invaded the dominions of Huascar. The latter marched against him with an army; but the younger and more warlike Atahuallpa had won the hearts of his veterans, and the elder was defeated. The battle was fought at Tumebamba, one of Huascar's cities, the inhabitants of which were all put to the sword by the revengeful Atahuallpa. Driven back towards Cuzco, Huascar rallied his troops for the defence of their sacred capital, and another and more terrible battle took place, in which he was utterly defeated and taken prisoner.

IX

A MARCH TO THE MOUNTAINS

1532

WE left Pizarro at San Miguel, that first town founded by Europeans in Peru, on the river Piura, not far from the sea. While he was engaged in partitioning lands and natives among the settlers, erecting buildings, and establishing a form of government, Atahuallpa the victorious was encamped in a beautiful valley at the base of the great mountains known as Cassamarca. He himself had not taken part in the last battle, for it had been fought and won by a brave general in command of his veteran troops.

As Cassamarca was conveniently situated between the far-distant cities of Quito and Cuzco - which latter the Inca had not yet seen - he awaited the coming of his general there, intending after his arrival to march upon the City of the Sun. His camp, in fact, was about ten days' journey from San Miguel, from which, in the last week of September, 1532, Pizarro set out to seek him. As will be shown in the unfolding of this narrative, Pizarro could not have chosen a more opportune time for invasion, or have contrived a more fortunate combination of circumstances, had he been perfectly aware of what was occurring behind that mysterious barrier of mountains which interposed between him and the army of the Inca. The death of Huayna Capac, the elder Inca, had occurred sometime in 1525, and while Pizarro was equipping himself for the conquest – reconnoitering the coast, voyaging to Spain and soliciting the crown, raising troops, accumulating munitions, and building vessels – the important events were happening within the empire, or kingdom, which were to hasten its downfall.

The decisive event, the conflict between Atahuallpa and Huascar, occurred in the first half of the year 1532, and but for that clash of the two sovereigns, who should have been at peace, Pizarro might not have been permitted to invade their country. For, not only had it weakened the Inca's power, by causing an alienation of hitherto servile thousands, whose allegiance was now divided, but it had been the cause of Atahuallpa's leaving his capital city of Quito and advancing to a point much nearer the coast, and hence more accessible to the invaders. Had there been no feud between the two rivals, on the thrones of Quito and Cuzco, and especially if they could have united against the common foe, there is no question but that the Spaniards would have been repelled, if not annihilated.

Many thousand Peruvians had been slain in battle, and the surly survivors compelled to look upon the victor as their lord; while in addition to the massacre committed by the soldiers, Atahuallpa had perpetrated another, by which the royal family of nobles was nearly exterminated. Summoning them to meet at Cuzco for consultation, it is said, he ordered them to be butchered, many to be tortured, merely because they could, like himself, boast of Inca blood in their veins. Many of them were his half-brothers, for the late Huayna Capac left a numerous progeny, "who might each one of them show a better title to the crown than the illegitimate Atahuallpa"; and many, again, were his sisters and cousins. All were regarded by the common people with veneration, and though these were the most submissive, docile subjects in the world, they could not but resent this bloody act of the usurper.

Another thing that contributed towards the weakness of the resistance encountered by Pizarro was the status of the people inhabiting many places on and near the coast. In pursuance of the Peruvian method, such of the places as had been recently conquered were governed by curacas, or caciques taken from the subjugated people, and, as may be imagined, these were not overzealous in defence of their master's dominions. Such were the curacas of Puná, Tumbez, and other cities, met with by the Spaniards in their march to the interior.

These, then, were the conditions that favored the Spaniards at the particular time they landed on the coast and invaded the country: internecine strife, which had resulted in the overthrow of the legitimate sovereign; universal distrust among the people, who had seen their revered ruler defeated in battle, made prisoner, and another advanced to the throne; and, finally, the easily diverted allegiance of the frontier inhabitants of a territory remote from the royal capital and centres of influence.

These things opened the way for Pizarro's advance, but they can hardly he said to have made possible the conquest of a country containing, perhaps, millions of people, whose warriors were numbered by the hundred thousand, and trained to blindly obey a despot who had never known defeat. They were imperfectly armed, it is true, with barbaric weapons, did not know the uses of gunpowder, were unacquainted with horses and cavalry, and could only oppose their thinly clad or naked bodies to the soldiers encased in steel armor. But they could assemble overwhelming masses, and were adepts at ambuscade and in the defence of mountain passes, through which the invaders would be compelled to march.

While the young Inca may have had an inkling of what was occurring on the coast, doubtless having received reports from Tumbez and Puná, he was in the dark as to the prowess of those who were soon to be his opponents. Vague reports had reached both Atahuallpa and Pizarro, by which both had been greatly disturbed. The Inca had heard of the wonderful weapons carried by the Spaniards, of the strange and terrible animals they rode, and of the shining armor they wore, which was impenetrable by arrow, dart, or javelin.

On the other hand, Pizarro had been informed by his interpreters of the invincible Inca, at whose nod myriads of fierce warriors were assembled in battle array, at whose behest thousands would offer themselves in sacrifice, going to death as joyfully as to a feast. But he was also told that this Inca possessed treasure incalculable, palaces plated with gold, and gems of inestimable value, which would become the spoil of the conqueror who should penetrate to his sacred capital of Cuzco.

That decided Pizarro, who resolved to wait no longer. Without the reinforcements he had expected, and for which he had delayed departure from San Miguel, he set out with less than two hundred men, to subdue a country containing a thousand times the number of his soldiers in a single province alone. First, there was a desert to cross; but the soldiers, refreshed by their long sojourn in the valley of the Piura, made nothing of it, and were rewarded for their toils when they turned towards the sierras by entering a fertile and picturesque country, well watered and abounding in fruits and flowers. Valleys of great beauty were found by the Spaniards, nestling among the hills and embosomed in the mountains, which, the farther they travelled, grew more and more difficult of ascent.

All the way, however, the army marched over one of the great royal roads, which, though at last winding and zigzagging among cliffs and crags, at times merely a narrow trail along the brinks of precipices, was smooth, and for the greater part shaded, with sparkling streams running beside the parapets.

It may not have been the Inca's intention to provide sustenance for the invaders of his country, but this he did, nevertheless. Every night, after entering the rough sierra region, they were sheltered beneath the roofs of the royal road-houses, and their meals were furnished from the ample

PERUVIAN WARRIORS

stores of provisions contained in adjacent granaries. This was "quartering on the enemy" with a vengeance, and grim Pizarro smiled as he reflected upon the manner in which his mission was being expedited by the very people he had come to conquer. Having received no orders to the contrary, these people wasted upon the invading Spaniards a gracious hospitality which was new in their experience, and which they basely requited.

At a little hamlet called Zaran, set in the centre of a mountain valley, the curaca received Pizarro so hospitably that he resolved to tarry here, while his lieutenant, De Soto, went on ahead with a small force to reconnoitre. De Soto was a dependable soldier, but, as the days lengthened into a week, and he did not return, his commander became uneasy. He was about setting out in search of him, when the cavalier appeared, his force intact, and in his company an Indian of imposing presence, a brother of the Inca himself, who had come as an ambassador. Like the messengers from Montezuma to Cortés, he brought rich presents for the stranger who had so rashly invaded his country, in the shape of a fountain carved from an emerald, gold-embroidered garments, and a peculiar perfume made from dried goose flesh. These he presented Pizarro, at the same time saying, through the interpreter, "Great stranger, I am here with a request from my sovereign and brother, the only and invincible Inca of Peru, that you honor him with your presence at his camp near Cassamarca, where the hot springs gush forth from the mountains."

"I have come for that purpose," replied Pizarro, without an instant's delay. "I and my comrades have come to see with our own eyes the great monarch of this land and to carry him a message from my own sovereign who is a still greater one, and who has laid upon me his commands to inform the king, your brother, the lord of this land, of the religion we profess, and to convert him to the practise of it, so that his soul may be saved from hell, in which, otherwise, it shall burn forever and forever!"

The ambassador made no reply, though he appeared astonished and incredulous that any people should have been so foolish as to come so far to impose their religion upon another people who already had one. He was shown about the camp and entertained at dinner, during which he expressed great satisfaction at the viands, and especially the wines, both food and drink being new to his palate. He examined everything he saw with attention, never before having seen either white men or their belongings, and was so insistent upon being told by the interpreters the meaning of it all that Pizarro was convinced that he came less as an ambassador than as a spy. He sent him away, however, without disclosing his suspicions, after presenting him with a red cap and a few glass beads, and with a message to the Inca that, having heard of his renown, he had come to assist him to subdue his enemies, as well as to convert him to the "only true faith." The Indian noble was delighted with the cap and beads, and so well pleased with all he saw that he must have made a most favorable report, for the Spaniards were not retarded in their march, but, rather, helped along, by royal orders. Was it the purpose of the Inca to lure the Spaniards on, deeper and deeper into the mountainous interior, and having secured the passes by which they had gained access to the country, fall upon and massacre them all? Or was he really animated by a curiosity to see for himself these wonderful strangers of whom he had heard so much? Pizarro was puzzled, but, true Spaniard that he was, inclined to a belief in the Inca's treachery rather than his good faith. He knew that he was placing himself in the Inca's power, provided treachery were intended; but he would not retreat, nor would he halt longer by the way. Sending back to San Miguel the presents he had received, not only from the Inca, but from the chiefs of various provinces, Pizarro gave the word to march onward. The place where the Inca was said to be encamped with his army was then but four or five days' distant, though the way was rugged and defended by forts. Owing to some oversight, these forts were not occupied, all the natives having been draughted into the Inca's army. Towns and villages were passed by, embedded in the vegetation of most fruitful valleys; but they were almost deserted, for the men were off in the army, and the women and children had fled to the forests.

A cluster of villages was discovered on the opposite bank of a broad and rapid river, to cross which Pizarro made a floating bridge, upon which all went over in safety, the cavaliers holding their horses by the bridles as they swam behind. No soldier of the company worked harder than Pizarro, who insisted upon remaining behind until the last of his men had passed over. By such acts as these, by "putting his shoulder to the wheel" whenever needed, and by constant oversight of his men, he won their regard; and they held to him loyally, undeterred by the prospect of danger ahead or the unknown fate that awaited them.

Hearing conflicting reports as to the strength of the Inca's army and the location of his camp, Hernando Pizarro obtained what he believed was the truth by putting a captive Indian to the torture. Under the pressure of a cord about his temples, twisted so tightly that his eyes nearly burst from their sockets, the poor wretch "confessed" that the Inca had revealed his plans to him, which were: to get the white men in his power, after decoying them so far into the country that they should be wholly at his mercy, then make slaves of them and appropriate their horses and their weapons. Almost any sort of a confession could have been obtained by torture, which, though it gratified the brutal passions of the Spaniards, rarely served their purpose at the time it was applied. This is only one cruel incident of a journey which lasted many days, and during which, doubtless, many another Indian was tortured, in order that he should be forced to reveal what he did not know!

After sending forward the curaca of San Miguel to ascertain if the mountain passes were guarded, Pizarro diverged from the great main road which he had been following for days, and took a narrower, more tortuous one, that led him and his band up the craggy sides of the cordillera. A mighty wall of mountains now opposed his progress, behind which, he was informed, lay the beautiful vale of Cassamarca, where he had every reason to believe, he would find the Inca and his army.

But it was one thing to know where the Inca was intrenched, and quite another to enter his stronghold! It was defended by a natural barrier which, had the Inca but supplemented the creations of nature with defensive works, and manned them with his soldiers, might have held the Spaniards off indefinitely. But, though at times the roadway was like the steps of a staircase cut in the solid rock, and several craggy points were met with which were crowned by fortresses, the Spaniards encountered no opposition in their passage of the cordillera.

At last, they reached the crest, where, benumbed by the cold, they might still have fallen easy victims to the valor of the Inca, if he had but put forth his arm to destroy. That he did not man the mountain passes with his best warriors, and from the craggy heights tumble down great rocks upon the heads of the ascending Spaniards, was taken as a proof that he had planned to kill them in some other way ; for, had he cared to do so, he might have swept them all into the sea.

X

IN THE INCA'S STRONGHOLD

1532

THE desperate nature of their venture must have been deeply impressed upon the Spaniards, as, climbing the slippery steps of that mountain roadway, the cavalry leading their horses by the bridles, and the infantry assisting their steps by means of pikes and arquebuses, they slowly progressed towards the sierra's summit. Carefully their scouts reconnoitred the craggy steeps, crowned by deserted fortresses, from which they expected an avalanche of rocks and stones and missile weapons. With every sense alert and nerves tingling with apprehension, they crept around the scarped sides of precipitous cliffs, now and then compelled to cross an abysmal chasm, over a frail and trembling suspension bridge of osiers, swung like a hammock above a roaring torrent.

They fully realized what it was they were now engaged in – the most perilous adventure of that century. Why were they climbing those mountain heights? Why were they penetrating the heart of a country swarming with inhabitants, as an ant-hill swarms with ants? Why were they suffering, enduring, persisting in going farther and farther into a region from which, if they were defeated in battle, there would be absolutely no escape?

Their leader, iron-hearted Pizarro, had from the first proclaimed their purpose to be the extension of their sovereign's power and the conversion of the Indians to the "only true faith"; but, if they ever admitted the truth, they could have confessed the real purpose of that expedition in a single word. It was *gold*, or its equivalent, that was the animating motive for all their toils and heroic exploits. But, while the motive was ignoble, no one can deny that they heroically endured, valiantly fought, and stoutly combated all the difficulties that man and nature had thrown in their way. They may have murmured, but no member of that little band complained aloud, for all the weak-kneed ones had been weeded out. Before the sierras were well entered, Pizarro had given them the opportunity to return to San Miguel. Only nine availed themselves of this offer, and the ninescore who remained were truly "men of blood and iron." They had borne their heavy armor beneath the blazing sun of the lowlands, sweltering and staggering with the heat and the burden; through the sierras they had toiled, upward, ever upward, and at last had arrived at the bleak plains, above which towered the higher Andes, with their crowns of perpetual ice and snow. While crossing this elevated region, with cold so intense that the soldiers shivered until their armor clanged, they were met by another embassy from the Inca. He sent greeting, and a gift of llamas to Pizarro; but his messenger was accused by a spy, who had penetrated to the Inca's camp and returned, of treachery on the part of his master. A wrangle ensued between the spy and the ambassador, during which it became evident to Pizarro that Atahuallpa was playing a double game, luring him on by gifts and fair promises, but all the while perfecting a snare for his destruction. It was but natural that Pizarro, himself with sinister aims against the monarch of the country he was invading, should hold suspicions of that sovereign; and again, it was not remarkable that the Inca should have viewed the approach of the Spaniards with distrust. In the simplicity of his nature, he saw no reason, no adequate motive, for this invasion, since he himself held gold in light esteem, and, content with the religion of his ancestors, could not conceive why the strangers should wish to impose their own upon him and his people.

A glorious vision burst upon the gaze of the Spaniards, when, having descended halfway the eastern declivities of the mountain range they had climbed, they saw the vale of Cassamarca spread before them. Oval in shape, about fifteen miles in length by three or four in width, verdant with a luxuriant vegetation and watered by sparkling streams, it lay amid the dark and frowning Andes like an emerald in a sombre setting. Through its fields and meadows ran a broad, deep river, which was spanned by two bridges of excellent construction, affording access to a small plateau at the foot of the sierras, where lay the white-walled city of Cassamarca.

The architecture of this city was of a composite character, for, while most of the dwellings were huts of sun-baked clay, and all were roofed with thatch of straw or palm, others again were of hewn stone and of massive construction. These latter, of course, gave Cassamarca its distinctive character, the most notable of them being a temple dedicated to the sun, the convents where dwelled the Virgins of the Sun, and huge barracks, in which the Inca's soldiers were usually quartered.

Two forts defended the place, one at the end of the plaza mentioned, and the other on higher ground, both constructed of hewn stone laid in massive blocks, the more elevated one reached by a winding stairway cut in the rock, and surrounded by a triple enclosure. So Cassamarca was a place

of great strength, and even though it had never before been visited or seen by white men, it was fortified, as though their coming had been long expected. There were other temples within the walls, besides the structure dedicated to the sun, and the city was well supplied with water by means of aqueducts, which also afforded irrigation facilities for the fields and gardens, thereby conducing to their aspect of exuberant fertility.

The chief attraction in this verdant valley, and which was probably the cause of the city having been built here, lay about three miles distant, and was indicated by the clouds of vapor hanging over it. Here were, and are to-day, the famous hot springs, to which the nobility and royalty of Peru resorted, and which Inca Atahuallpa was enjoying when rumors reached him of Pizarro's entrance into his kingdom. The slopes of the surrounding hills were covered with the tents of his army, which, an observer states, appeared in the distance like snow-flakes, so white and numerous were they.

In his richly hung pavilion, towards the close of a day in mid-November, sat Inca Atahuallpa, surrounded by his court. The pavilion was so pitched that access was afforded, on the one hand, to a spring of thermal water, and on the other to one of refreshing coolness fresh from the mountain. Numerous tents adjacent contained the nobles and their families, while others, almost equally numerous, held the inmates of the royal harem.

Amid the brilliantly clad courtiers and warriors, Atahuallpa was conspicuous, not alone by the dignity of his presence, but on account of the obsequious attention bestowed upon him, for none approached except with averted face and eyes cast to the ground. He was tall, even stately, for a Peruvian; his face was brown and beardless, his eyes black, glittering, and bloodshot; his jet-black hair was cut short, and around his head was twisted a turban of many colors, with a peculiar fringe hanging from it to the eyebrows. This head-dress was adorned with a plume which had been plucked from the *coraquenque*, a bird so rare that only two of the species were supposed to exist at the same time, and these were preserved to furnish the distinctive insignia of royalty. The fringe of crimson wool, called the *borla*, which almost concealed the Inca's eyes, except when he swept it aside with his hand, was another emblem of royalty, without which he could not appear in public. His chief garment was a large, loose robe of finest wool, brilliantly colored, and his adornments consisted of emeralds worn in profusion, finger-rings, ear-rings, and bracelets of gold.

Surrounded by his army, in whose strength he had so implicitly relied as to allow Pizarro to enter the valley without opposition, Atahuallpa considered himself invincible. Yet he was disturbed at the thought of the continuous advance of that mailed band of monsters now descending the slopes of the sierra. He could see their glittering arms and fluttering banners, as they reached the lower hills and wound out into the plain, and needed not the reports of his generals to convince him that they were marching straight upon Cassamarca. He had invited them thither, in truth, had emptied the city of its inhabitants, and the great halls of his soldiers, in order that they might find room in which to take up their quarters.

Marching in three divisions, and in order of battle, the undaunted warriors advanced without a halt across the valley and into the city, where they sought quarters in the barracks provided for the Indian soldiery. Each great building was more than a hundred feet in length, and divided into several apartments, with doors opening upon the square or plaza. An ominous silence greeted the Spaniards as they tramped through the deserted streets, and they looked in vain for some one to welcome them. But, though the city when occupied was said to have contained ten thousand inhabitants, not one seemed to have been left within its walls.

Whether this boded ill, or betokened an excess of hospitality, Pizarro knew not. The Inca assured him, later, that he had cleared the city in order that his guests might have the greatest liberty and feel that it was truly theirs. But the silence itself was ominous, and, suspecting that the fortress frowning over him might contain a body of warriors secreted within its walls, he ordered it to be occupied at once, himself climbing the stony steeps in the van of his men. From the parapet of the cliff-top fortress, he had an unobstructed view of the town and valley spread out beneath him, and also of the Inca's camp three miles away.

Descending swiftly, he disposed his troops according to a plan which he had conceived while gazing down upon the valley. He had discovered nothing at all suspicious, either in the Inca's movements or in the city and its environs; but he still believed Atahuallpa was concerting some deep-laid scheme for his destruction, and resolved to anticipate him. From the moment of his descent, in truth, events shaped by his actions, set in motion by the operations of his powerful mind, succeeded each other with such rapidity, that, though it was then late in the afternoon, before darkness fell next day he had virtually accomplished the conquest of Peru.

This seems incredible; but the sober statements of historians bear us out in this assertion. Though Pizarro had been for years intent upon and preparing for the conquest; though he had been for months engaged in this campaign and for weeks on the march, the capture of the Inca, carrying with it the subjugation of his myriad subjects, was but a matter of hours. Hurried on by the dæmon within him, now that the crucial moment had arrived, Pizarro made his moves with dexterity and rapidity.

A storm of hail and snow had greeted his arrival at Cassamarca,[1] but that did not delay his arrangements, nor deter him from sending a body of cavalry, under De Soto and Hernando Pizarro, to announce his arrival to the Inca and request his commands. The descending sun had reached the crest of the western sierra ere the little band of cavaliers started on this perilous mission, but they put spurs to their steeds and were soon in the presence of Atahuallpa. A trumpeter rode in the van and announced their progress by loud blasts which resounded throughout the valley, so that the Inca was apprised of their coming, and gave orders for his warriors to admit them within the lines. His attitude and that of his nobles was friendly, but that of the warriors seemed hostile, for all had arms in their hands, such as spears and lances, bows and arrows. Had they chosen to do so, they might easily have annihilated these thirty-five bold horsemen; though it would have cost them dear, for each man was the pick of his company, and stouter hearts never beat in human breasts than those of the two Hernandos, De Soto, and Pizarro.

[1] Cajamarca, Caxamarca, or, more literally, Cassamarca, probably received its name from *cassa*, hail, and *marca*, a province, owing to the frequency with which it was visited by sleety storms.

The Inca was discovered half reclining on a cushion, surrounded by his nobles, ranged according to their respective rank. They parted, as the horsemen approached, and Hernando Pizarro, without dismounting, but respectfully doffing his helmet, announced through an interpreter the object of his visit. It was the same old speech, which, placed in the mouths of various desperadoes, had done service in Mexico and elsewhere, to wit: "We have come, O mighty prince, in the name of a still mightier monarch across the great waters, who, having heard of you and your wonderful country, has been moved to send this embassy, in order to cultivate your friendship, and especially to impart to you the doctrines of the only true faith, which we profess, and without which you and your subjects shall be condemned to flames everlasting. We have also come with an invitation from our commander, who would be pleased to have you visit him without delay, but who awaits your orders."

II

Having delivered his message, Hernando awaited an answer, but it did not come. During all the interview the Inca had remained with his gaze directed to the ground, and had not deigned to cast even a glance at the cavaliers. He had spoken not a word nor seemed to hear the message; but finally, after an interval of silence, one of his nobles inclined his head and muttered, "It is well." But still, though tacitly invited to depart, the Spaniards had not learned the Inca's pleasure, and their spokesman pressed for a reply. A faint smile flickered across Atahuallpa's features as he at last found voice and replied: "This is a fast-day, and I must keep it rigidly, but to-morrow I will visit your commander and inform him of my pleasure. Meanwhile, let him occupy the great buildings on the plaza till I come."

As he glanced, though somewhat listlessly, at the horse De Soto rode, that cavalier, said to have been the best mounted in the army, thought to astonish, if not to terrify, the Inca by putting the fiery steed through his paces. Clapping the spurs into its sides, he caused the mettlesome charger to prance and rear, to dash furiously forward upon the plain, and then to return at full speed, straight for the Inca and assembled nobles.

Atahuallpa had never seen a horse before that day, and may have been excused if he thought it some unearthly monster with an appetite for human blood; but when it charged directly for him, and even when thrown upon its haunches so close that flecks of foam bespattered the royal robes, he manifested no fear. So stolid and unfeeling was he, in fact (according to Pedro Pizarro), that several of his warriors, who had shrunk back in fear, were ordered by him to be executed!

XI

HOW ATAHUALLPA WAS CAPTURED

1532

THE cavaliers were invited to dismount and partake of refreshments; but as it was late they were in haste to return, and accepted only a foaming beverage called *chicha*, which was handed up to them by dark-skinned Hebes, and which they drank from golden goblets gemmed with emeralds. Their fingers itched to snatch those precious vessels from the fair hands of the Indian maidens, and bear them back as trophies to their commander; but they forebore – the time was not yet come for pillage.

They rode back to camp in the darkness, the white road showing them the way, gloomily discussing the strength and martial aspect of the Inca's army. They were now convinced of his power, as well as of the grandeur of his court, and were more than dubious as to the result should he appeal to arms. Their fears they communicated to Pizarro, who, though he also realized the critical nature of their situation, affected to scoff at their misgivings.

"Fear ye not," he exclaimed. "Have I not known this all the time? Have I not been dwelling upon this situation by night and by day? And, think ye, comrades, that I have not a scheme? Ay, that have I. This is it. Listen, attend, and obey, for all our lives depend upon the success of it!"

They were gathered within the fortress on the height, where Pizarro had posted their artillery, consisting of two falconets, or small field-pieces, in charge of Pedro de Candia. The cavalry were quartered in the barracks, the infantry in the "House of the Serpent"; sentinels paced their rounds in the upper and the lower fortress. All due care having been taken to secure the camp against surprise, Pizarro and his captains had assembled for a council of war.

"I hold that we are of one mind," continued Pizarro, "which is that ours is a most desperate case. Whatever happens, whichever way we turn, we cannot retreat. Neither can we go forward, nor stay still. We cannot engage the army of the Inca in the open field – it is too vast. We might hold our own here for a time, if attacked; but we have only a scanty supply of provisions, and even this is owing to the bounty of the Inca.

There is only one thing to do. I have pondered it long, but only this day did it appear to me how it could be done. What think ye it is, brothers and comrades?"

No one replied, for each one feared to guess aright, as that would have vexed their commander.

"Ha! you cannot imagine? No, of course not. But I, Francisco Pizarro, though it is said I cannot read nor write – I can think! And this is what I have thought: that no thing, no man, no beast, nor government can live without a head! Cut off the head, and you cut down the man, beast, or government – you take its life ! Well, we cut off the head of Peru at a stroke by –"

"Beheading Atahuallpa the Inca," exclaimed his three brothers, almost in unison.

"Nay, nay," answered Francisco, with a smile. "At least, not until we have him in hand. But that is it – to take him!"

"But how?" It was De Soto who asked the question. He had no doubt of his commander's ability to accomplish anything he undertook, and he knew, also, that whenever the slow-thinking Pizarro declared his thoughts he was ready to strike.

"Well," answered Pizarro, "our artillery is here, in the fortress, the cavalry in barracks at one side of the plaza; the foot-soldiers are in quarters opposite. Now, then, Atahuallpa the Inca comes to-morrow – let it be with a force large or small, it matters not; he comes, he enters the plaza. At the signal of command, which I will give when ready, the cavalry fall upon the throng in front of them; the foot-soldiers, the pikemen and the arquebusiers do likewise on their side; the falconets in the fortress play upon the army outside the walls and put them to rout. That is all. The plan is simple, it is feasible, and it shall be carried out. But one thing, remember: the Inca must not be killed. With him in our hands, and alive, we have the strongest assurance of safety; but once he dies – that is the end of us!"

The council discussed the scheme till long past the midnight hour, and in the end unanimously favored it. Whether the Inca intended treachery or no, absolute safety could only be assured them by depriving him of liberty, perhaps of life. They felt sure the Inca had a grievance, that his coming boded them ill, for he had told the interpreter that one of his curacas, Maygabilica, had sent him an iron collar which the Spaniards had placed around the neck of another curaca, whom they had maltreated shamefully; he had also informed him that the Spaniards were not immortal, not even puissant warriors, for he had killed three of them and one of their horses. When the army with which his generals had defeated Huascar arrived, they would drive the Spaniards from the country. Meanwhile, he would entertain them in Cassamarca, and on the morrow he would visit them in state.

The Spaniards were awake and alert with the morning sun, which, rising bright and clear, was hailed by the Peruvians as a propitious omen. The Inca's camp was early astir, and within the city walls all was commotion, also, among the Spaniards. Arms and armor were furbished to a mirrorlike brightness, the harness of the cavalry was hung with bells, arquebuses were charged, and the cannon in the fortress trained to sweep the plain. After a bountiful breakfast, mass was said, and prayers were offered, in which God's blessing was invoked upon the projected massacre of men made in His image! – for most of the atrocious deeds of the Spaniards were committed in the name of religion, and sanctioned by the priests who accompanied the army. The soldiers chanted a hymn, and then, "filled with a holy zeal for the conversion of the heathen," took the posts assigned them by their captains.

The day wore on, but, despite the activity prevailing in the Inca's camp, nothing seemed to come of it save bustle and confusion. No advance was made in the morning, and noon arrived before the march was actually begun. A multitude of Indians poured forth upon the highway, in the van being a corps of menials who swept it clean for the passage of their immaculate monarch, borne in a palanquin upon the shoulders of stalwart chiefs, the most conspicuous personage in the procession. Immediately behind him marched a body-guard of picked warriors, who, in accordance with a message sent by the Inca to Pizarro, were all well armed. The Spaniards had come to his camp, said Atahuallpa, with weapons in their hands, consequently his men would appear in like manner.

Pizarro had returned answer that it mattered not to him how they came, so he received a visit from their great sovereign, whom he was anxious to meet and entertain. All the more anxious, was he, now that the afternoon waned, with Atahuallpa still on the road. Less than a mile from the city, however, the procession halted, while the soldiers that occupied the highway, and those who marched by thousands on either flank, separated into groups as if about to pitch their tents and form a camp. No doubt of this intention was allowed to linger in the mind of Pizarro, after a messenger from Atahuallpa arrived, with the intelligence that his royal master had concluded to remain where he was for the night, but would proceed again in the morning.

This was astounding news to Pizarro and his soldiers, who had then been chafing at their posts since break of day. They were tired, they were hungry to desperation, and consequently they were greatly incensed against Atahuallpa. What an unreasonable Inca he was, to be sure, and how unstable! He surely deserved his fate, whatever was preparing for him, for no man like that, who did not know his own mind two hours at a time, was fit to govern a kingdom!

The situation at this moment cannot fail to suggest the fable of the "spider and the fly." The amiable Pizarro represents the dissembling spider, who, having spread his web in a convenient corner, awaits with impatience the coming of his victim.

But the shallow-pated Atahuallpa, though unable to fathom the deeps of Pizarro 's perfidy, is yet uneasy. Why, he asks himself (and perhaps his nobles have also ventured to inquire, in their humble way), should he walk into the web at all?

Why, indeed? It was certainly incredibly foolish in him to do so. He had nothing at all to gain, but, on the contrary, everything to lose, by entering the city at that time.

It is impossible, at this distance from the time and circumstance, for us to penetrate the motives of the Inca – if he had any – and, in fact, no adequate explanation has ever been given for his advance into the heart of his enemy's camp. Perhaps he may have had an overweening confidence in his prowess, never having met any opponent who could overthrow him, and having been taught from earliest childhood to believe himself invincible and infallible.

But, the net having been spread since dawn, Pizarro was exceedingly vexed that Atahuallpa should hesitate to walk directly into it and promptly entangle himself. He sent back word that, having prepared a banquet against the coming of the Inca, he should certainly expect him to sup with him that night. As it was already late, he would suggest that his highness keep on, and enter the city while the sun was yet above the mountains.

What the impelling reason was, no one may ever know, but doubtless it was the dominant mind of Pizarro acting upon the feebler will of the Inca; at all events, the latter again changed his intention, and at once announced to his generals that he would pass the night in Cassamarca. The sun had almost set when, preceded by the band of menials in their checkered robes of red and white, and by groups of musicians playing on rude instruments, singing, and dancing, battalions of warriors began to file into the square. They were arrayed in garments of many colors, on their breasts were great plates of gold, on their heads tiger-skin helmets studded with gems, and in their hands maces of copper and silver. Beneath their tunics, it was afterwards charged by the Spaniards, they carried slings and darts, for an emergency; but if so, they made no use of them. Company after company marched in, until the plaza was alive with Indians – almost filled, in truth. They lined it many deep, deploying into two great bodies, so that, when a wild burst of barbaric music announced the approach of the Inca, the magnificent prince and his gorgeous escort, blazing with gems and with nodding plumes, passed through a living lane of warriors. High over all, seated in a throne of massive gold adorned with parrots' plumes, the "Child of the Sun" gazed serenely and unmoved upon the vast assemblage. He was more gorgeously arrayed than when visited by the cavaliers, for besides the blood-red borla fringe that hid his brow, and the rare feathers in his diadem, he wore a broad collar of emeralds, and his voluminous robe blazed with jewels. As the palanquin and its escort reached the centre of the square, Atahuallpa ordered a halt and looked around him. He saw on every side the eager, upturned faces of his people; but, save for a small group of cavaliers gathered about Pizarro in a corner of the plaza, no

Spaniards were in sight.

"Where are they, where are the strangers?" he asked, in surprise. As if in answer to his question, a strangely garbed figure advanced from the corner, and, approaching the Inca, held up a crucifix before him. It was Pizarro's chaplain, Friar Vicente Valverde, and as he stood there silent, in his cowl, with rope – begirdled robe and sandaled feet, Atahuallpa gazed at him in astonishment.

He had come to see Pizarro, the captain of the stranger band; but this could not be he, for his appearance was not martial, like that of the cavaliers who had visited him in camp. One of the nobles who had met Pizarro in the mountains was standing near the litter, and of him Atahuallpa inquired what office this man held. He replied, it is said, that he was the Spaniards' "guide of talk and priest of their supreme deity." The rest were not like him, he added, but in a certain sense he was their captain.

While the Inca was puzzling over this answer, the monk opened his mouth and poured forth such a discourse as (it is safe to say) no Child of the Sun had ever listened to before. Various renderings have been given of this discourse, but probably the most literal is that of the historian Benzoni, who was in Peru a few years later, and had it directly from the lips of the conquerors. Coming to the Inca's entry into Cassamarca, he says: "Ataballba (Atahuallpa) thus entered triumphantly into the city, feeling quite safe, to hear the messages of the bearded men. Brother Vicente Valverde, of the order of St. Dominic, with cross and breviary in his hand, advanced to the presence of his majesty, as if to make that monarch believe that he had some great theologian before him. By means of the interpreter, he gave him to understand that he came to his excellency commissioned by his sacred majesty, the emperor, with the authority of the Roman pontiff, celestial vicar of our Saviour, who had given him the unknown countries so that he might send there worthy persons to preach and to publish His most holy name, doing away with their (the Peruvians') false and diabolical errors.

"Thus saying, he showed him the Law of God (the Bible), and related how He had created all out of nothing. He related the beginning of Adam and Eve, and how Jesus Christ descended from heaven and became incarnate; how He then died on the cross, and rose again to redeem mankind. Having then reascended to heaven, He confirmed the resurrection of the dead and the life of Peter, His first vicar. Brother Valverde then showed the authority of the pontiffs, Peter's successors, and finally the authority of the emperor and King of Spain, monarch of the world. He concluded with showing the Inca that it was his duty to become a friend and tributary of the emperor, submitting to the divine law and the Christian religion, and abandoning his false gods. 'And if you do not accede to this, war will compel you to it!' concluded Brother Valverde.

"When the Inca heard this he said in reply that he would certainly live in friendship with the 'monarch of the world'; but it did not seem incumbent upon a free king, like himself, to pay tribute to a person he had never seen, and that the pontiff must be a great fool to give away so liberally the property of others! As to religion: he would on no account abandon his own, for if they believed in Christ, who died on the cross, he believed in the Sun, who never died.

"Then he asked Valverde how he knew that the god of the Christians had made the world from nothing, and that he had died on the cross. The monk answered that the Book said so, handing the Bible to Ataballba, who took it, and after looking at it laughed, and said, 'This says nothing to me.' He then threw it on the ground, whence the monk took it back again, and immediately called out with a loud voice: 'Vengeance! vengeance, Christians! for the gospels are despised and thrown on the ground! You may now kill these dogs who despise the Law of God!'

"Francisco Pizarro, having unfurled his flags, gave the order for battle. Thus the first guns were fired, and immediately on this alarm the horses followed, with bells round their necks and on their legs, making great noise withal, and adding to the crashing of the guns, the trumpets, and the drums. Laying hands on their weapons, the Spaniards then attacked the Indians, who, stupefied by so much novelty, by such ferocious animals, and by the sharpness of their swords, began to clear away and fly in utter disorder."

What can we add to this account, by one who had conversed with the participants in this dreadful affray? It would seem that perfidy could go no further, for, whatever might have been the outcome of the monk's appeal to Atahuallpa, Pizarro had resolved upon his capture and the [12] massacre of his subjects. These hypocrites, who cloaked their designs in the garb of religion, were about to stain with blood the holy emblems which they had held up for the Inca to worship. Shouting the well-known battle-cry, "Santiago! Santiago!" Pizarro gave the signal for slaughter. The cavalry burst out upon the defenceless Indians like a band of demons, cutting and slashing, bearing down all before them, crushing the poor creatures beneath iron hoofs, and carrying consternation everywhere. On the other side, they were attacked by the infantry, shot down by the musketeers and cross-bowmen, lanced by the halberdiers, and brained with ponderous battle-axes.

There was no resistance, for the Indians were not only unarmed, but were taken completely by surprise. On every side blood flowed like water in a freshet; but it was Indian blood, for scarcely a drop escaped from Spanish veins that day. As the foot-soldiers and cavalry advanced towards one another, hewing their way through the quivering ranks of unresisting Indians, the Inca and his escort became the centre of conflict. Around the royal litter, still upheld by faithful attendants, gathered the frantic chiefs and nobles, offering their lives in a vain attempt to save, or for a while defend, their revered sovereign. They were cut down ruthlessly, and a mound of writhing, bleeding bodies was formed about the litter, which, deprived of its support, crashed to the ground. As Atahuallpa fell he was set upon by a soldier, who would have despatched him instantly had not Pizarro, at that moment, thrust forth his sword, receiving a slight wound in the hand. Throwing the soldier to one side, he shouted: "The Inca shall not be slain! Let no harm come to him, on pain of death!"

THE CAPTURE OF ATAHUALLPA

He himself seized the unhappy monarch by the arm, while the soldier, balked of his prey, in revenge snatched the imperial borla from his brow and bore it off in triumph. The plaza was filled with the sounds of strife: the clashing of weapons, the cries of the wounded, and shouts of the soldiery; while over all hung a pall of smoke, from the incessant fire of cannon and musketry. Dazed by the terrible occurrences about him, stupefied by his sudden descent from the pinnacle of earthly greatness to the depths of humiliation, Atahuallpa was led away by Pizarro and delivered over to a guard.

As the news of his capture spread around, the Peruvians were seized with a panic, and a large body of them burst through a wall surrounding the enclosure and fled into open country. They were pursued by the cavalry and cut down remorselessly, while of the five thousand warriors who had accompanied the Inca, at least half their number lay rigid in death, or bleeding from ghastly wounds.

So perfectly was the scheme of Pizarro carried out that the bloody work consumed less than an hour. The Inca had entered the plaza shortly before set of sun. When darkness fell he had lost his empire, his army was in flight, and his life at the mercy of the enemy.

XII

THE PRISONER AND HIS RANSOM

1532

RECALLED by shrill blasts of the trumpet, the cavalry ceased their pursuit of the fugitives, and returned to the plaza, where the last scenes of the dreadful massacre were enacted in the despatching of the wounded and the removal of the dead. While the pavement of the plaza was still encumbered with the victims of the Spaniards' vengeance, the Inca was summoned from his cell to sup with his conqueror. Pizarro might have spared his prisoner this humiliation, but his nature was of the coarse and vulgar sort that gloats over the condition of a fallen foe. Atahuallpa had been roughly handled in the affray at the litter, and his robes torn from his person, so he was re-clothed in less expensive garments, while his diadem and jewels were appropriated by the victor.

In the accounts given of this banquet following after the massacre, it is stated that the Inca bore himself with serenity, though still bewildered by the sudden and terrible change in his fortunes. Like Montezuma of Mexico, in similar circumstances, he accepted his hard fate stoically, and even indulged in the hope of an early release from imprisonment. But, with all his fortitude, he had, as may be imagined, but little appetite for the tempting viands that were set before him, nor would he more than taste the delicious wines in which Pizarro besought him to drown the remembrance of his woes.

It was veritably a "Barmecide feast" for the unfortunate Atahuallpa, who might well have thought it all unreal and but the product of a dream. He was brought to his senses, however, by Pizarro, who improved the occasion by delivering a homily upon his pride and arrogance; and he did not fail to mention how fortunate Atahuallpa should consider himself in having fallen into the hands of such considerate people as the Spaniards and such a merciful captain as himself. "Reflect," he said, "upon what you did. You came against us with a mighty army; you threw the Book of God upon the ground; you insulted a minister of the Most High; yet we have preserved your life, and have killed but a few hundred of your people. This punishment, you cannot but perceive, has been sent in order that you should be abased, and be forced to acknowledge the greatness of our Lord and God, in whom we believe."

Atahuallpa humbly assented, amazed at himself that he should accept the commands of this low-born conqueror. He could not but admit that the gods of the strangers were more powerful than his own, though he was inclined to attribute his downfall to the fortunes of war and not to the defection of his gods. To the end, indeed, he clung to his belief in the sun -god, and gave adherence to no other.

Conquered and conqueror, that night, slept in a room of the great "Serpent House," and guarded by some of the sentinels whom Pizarro, with his customary watchfulness, had posted throughout the plaza and surrounding buildings. The Spanish captain did not seek his couch until he had taken every precaution against a surprise by the enemy, who, even though dispersed and demoralized, might yet rally and again brave death in an attempt to rescue their revered sovereign.

But the night – that memorable night of November 16, 1532 – passed without disturbance, and the morning sun once more shone brightly upon the vale and city of Cassamarca. The day was the Sabbath, yet it was not to be one of rest or recreation, for either Spaniards or Peruvians, as both were actively employed, the former in scouring the plain for prisoners, and the latter in removing the corpses of those who had been slain in the massacre.

A body of cavalry went out to ransack the Inca's camp at the hot springs, and in the afternoon returned with immense booty in gold and jewels, besides several thousand prisoners, including the entire household of Atahuallpa, not excepting the favorite members of his harem. Those whom the Inca desired were allowed to attend him, and he was given quarters large enough to accommodate all, where his privacy would not be invaded.

In the composite nature of Pizarro, cruelty and the humane sentiment were strangely blended. While on occasions he could be as cruel as Atahuallpa himself – in whom in-born ferocity was always slumbering – yet again he was often moved to merciful deeds. He was the only Spaniard wounded at the massacre, yet he seemed to bear no ill-will, either towards the soldier who had inadvertently slashed him with his sword, or against the Inca, whom he was defending at the moment. So, when some of his men approached him with a proposition for putting the prisoners to death, or maiming them by cutting off their hands, to prevent them from doing further harm, he rejected it without hesitation. He had shed blood enough already to awe the natives and prevent them from rising against the Spaniards; though there still existed an army of many thousand Peruvians, besides the fugitives then fleeing to the mountains.

Although prepared, by what they had seen, for an immense amount of plunder in the Inca's camp and pleasure pavilion, what they secured there surprised the Spaniards greatly. They brought back golden cups and goblets, ewers, urns, vases, bracelets, necklaces, and emeralds by the handful, all of which, together with the spoil stripped from the nobles murdered in the plaza, were deposited in safekeeping for future division. Vast droves of llamas, the Peruvian sheep, were found wandering on the hills, in charge of skilled shepherds, and hundreds of them were driven in and slaughtered for the table. Unaware of the strict regulations under which these large flocks had been accumulated, and by which they had been preserved, the Spaniards not only slaughtered these valuable animals indiscriminately, but allowed the survivors finally to run wild and disperse.

There were few things which the invaders had the capacity to appreciate at their real worth; but to gold, gems, fine feathers and fabrics they attached an exaggerated importance. Seeing and noting this, the shrewd Atahuallpa took hope that he might, perchance, purchase his freedom by appealing to Spanish avarice. One day, as he and Pizarro were conversing together, he let drop the remark that he could, if so inclined, cover with gold the floor of the room in which he was confined.

Pizarro 's dull eyes sparkled, observing which the Inca continued, "Not the floor only can I cover, but half the room I will fill, if – if you will but set me free."

The avaricious conqueror gasped in astonishment, but his habitual caution did not desert him. "That would be a vast treasure, surely," replied he, slowly; "but the cost would be great, i' faith!"

"The price would be my freedom; that is not much – to you; it is everything to me. But I will do more. See – as high as I can reach on the wall, this room will I fill with treasure of gold, and the room next this twice over with silver." Saying this, Atahuallpa the Inca stood on his toes and held his hand high against the wall.

Pizarro hesitated, not because he hoped to drive a better bargain; for never before had a ransom been offered so large, even for the life of a king. But he was reflecting upon the consequences to himself should the Inca be set free. The experiment would be worth trying, for he could thus get hold of treasure that might otherwise be secreted by the natives and be lost to him, and – he craftily reasoned with himself – he might give his word to free the Inca, and keep it, but quickly get his prisoner in the toils again. So he cried out heartily, with the air of an honest man, "I agree!" and sending for paint and a brush, he drew a red line along the wall, at the height indicated by the Inca. Some say it was nine feet above the floor; but, at any rate, it was as high as a man of medium size could reach, standing on tiptoe; and the room was thirty-five feet in length by eighteen in breadth.

That would be 35 x 18 x 7, let us say; so many cubic feet of gold! Not solid, not in nuggets and ingots, but in the form of ornaments, idols, plate, basins, ewers – worth many times their weight in gold as archæological treasures; but that the Spaniards did not know. After they got them in their possession, they broke up and cast into bars this inestimable treasure, and thus the world lost what can never be replaced.

Two months the Inca demanded for the collection of the ransom, for the most of it was in Cuzco, many days' distant by swift couriers, and a long and painful journey for the porters, bowed beneath their precious burdens. Orders were instantly sent to the capital, to Quito, and to the various depositories of the Inca's wealth, which were obeyed without question, and soon the golden stream was flowing towards the vale of Cassamarca.

The Peruvians valued the precious metals only for their use and ornament, while the Spaniards paid for them the price of their souls. They were willing to go through fire and flood for gold and silver, and jeopard their hopes of heaven in their acquisition. Gold was the "greatest thing in the world," for, according to their belief, it not only placed all the pleasures of earth within their grasp, but secured exemption from the pains of purgatory! Hence their avid desire to get it, the risks they ran to acquire it, whether rightfully or not, and the dangers they braved in its pursuit.

Soon the great highway between Cassamarca and Cuzco was alive with Indians staggering beneath their burdens of gold and silver. They arrived at Cassamarca, singly and in groups, with treasure to the amount of fifty thousand dollars daily; yet the greedy Spaniards, though they were looking upon a vaster spoil than any they had ever dreamed of finding, were dissatisfied. Their appetite grew with the means for gratifying it, and they began to complain of the Inca's dilatory methods.

Rumors arose of his intention to beguile them with a sight of treasure and false promises, while his armies were assembling, even on the road to Cassamarca. When taxed with this by Pizarro, Atahuallpa laughed in scorn. "Delay!" he cried. "Why should I delay? Is not my freedom worth more to me than aught else in the world? What can I do, a prisoner here, and my armies scattered all the way between Cuzco and Quito? You have only to send out spies, commander, to ascertain the truth. Do so, I beseech you, and you will learn that Atahuallpa keeps his word."

Pizarro did as suggested, and found no cause for alarm. In truth, he sent out his brother, Hernando, with a squadron, who reported all quiet in the country districts, and then pushed on to the town of Pachacamac, situated nearly three hundred miles away, in the mountains. This place was the abode of a deity worshipped by some of the Peruvians as the creator of the world. He belonged to a tribe of Indians that had been conquered by the Incas, and was so much revered by them that the sagacious sun-worshippers, instead of overthrowing his image and massacring his priests (as the Spaniards would have done), admitted him to a place in their pantheon. While they believed their religion to be the only true one, and their rulers heaven-descended children of the sun, they were not concerned about the gods of other peoples. If they chose to run after false gods, let them do so, and take the consequences. But in time, the Peruvian conquerors themselves came to regard the god of Pachacamac with veneration, and he was virtually admitted to conjoint worship with their own deity.

When he reached Pachacamac, Hernando Pizarro proceeded after the manner customary with the conquerors, and, being refused admission to the sanctuary, broke down the door, and found himself in a gloomy cave, "smelling like a slaughter-house." At the far end of the cavern the great idol was perceived, grinning at the Spaniards out of the darkness, and without further ceremony he was seized by the shoulders and ejected. When brought to the light he was discovered to be a hideous monster, in the form of a beast with the head of a man, carved out of wood. He was soon reduced to fragments, and after the cave had been cleansed a large stone cross was erected in his place, which the natives regarded with veneration, and cared for so faithfully that it remained there many years.

The Indians had everywhere received Hernando and his men with hospitality, and no sign of hostility had been perceived in any place; but, though they had regaled them with banquets by the way, and met them with music and dancing, they had forwarded to the priests of Pachacamac tidings as to the true mission of the strangers. Thus the priests had been forewarned, and, gathering their treasures together, had decamped for parts unknown.

It was a sore disappointment to the freebooters to find that the bulk of the treasure had been taken away, and they cursed their folly in first attending to matters of religion, instead of to the despoiling of the temple. Thereafter, they promised themselves they would first secure the plunder, and leave the destroying of idols and erecting of crosses to their spiritual advisers, whose business it was to attend to such things.

Notwithstanding their remissness, however, they managed to secure pillage to the amount of about a hundred thousand dollars, and obtained information at Pachacamac that was worth vastly more than that. This was, that the principal commander of the Inca's army in the south, the renowned Chalcuchima, was at a town in the vicinity with a small guard only, though not far away lay a body of his warriors, estimated at thirty or thirty-five thousand. Instead of offering battle, the general allowed himself to be approached by emissaries of Hernando, who assured him that it was the command of his master, Atahuallpa, that he return with them to Cassamarca. Now, Chalcuchima was the general who, in conjunction with another named Quizquiz (then at Cuzco), had won the great victory over Huascar Inca, by which Atahuallpa had been raised to supreme power in the empire. He was really a great commander, and, having almost unlimited resources under his control, including a large army of seasoned warriors, he might have met and vanquished, in all probability destroyed, the band of Spaniards under Hernando Pizarro. He had heard of the capture of his sovereign by a small body of wonderful warriors, and was burning to avenge the insult to his sacred majesty. But as time went by and no orders came from the head of the state, who alone could issue them, being the commander-in-chief, he was puzzled and bewildered.

When, then, a detachment from that band of invincible strangers made its way to his mountain stronghold, bearing a command for him to hasten back with them to see and converse [13] with the Inca, he accepted the order without distrust, and prepared to accompany Hernando Pizarro. He was borne in a litter on the shoulders of attendants, who served in relays, and at every place along the highway was received by the people with great ceremony; yet, on his arrival at Cassamarca, he abased himself before the Inca like the meanest of his countrymen. He entered the town in state, but when arrived at the plaza, alighted from his litter, put off his sandals and gold-embroidered robes, and, taking a burden on his back, in token of inferior station, went in and prostrated himself at Atahuallpa's feet. He kissed his hands repeatedly, and, with tears raining down his furrowed cheeks, exclaimed in a voice choking with emotion: "O my master! Would that I had been here: then this terrible misfortune might not have come to you."

But the Inca, though said to have been tenderly attached to Chalcuchima, manifested no emotion whatever. He could be gay and cordial with the Spaniards, but was ever haughty and dignified in converse with his subjects. He listened to him coldly, and then, without deigning to convey any information respecting his future plans, waved him away, with a gesture that signified there was still a "great gulf fixed" between even the greatest of his subjects and the "Child of the Sun." Chalcuchima departed sorrowfully; but this was only the first of his humiliations, for he was detained a prisoner by Pizarro, instead of being allowed to return to his army, and never recovered his freedom.

The roads and trails of the mountains were so rugged that the horses of Hernando Pizarro's troop lost their shoes long before the expedition was ended, and, there being no iron at hand, they were all shod with silver! That metal and gold were found to be abundant in the region around and beyond Pachacamac, and it was with this welcome information (as well as with his important prisoner) that Hernando returned to his brother, after an absence of nearly four months.

Meanwhile, successive events had brought matters near to a crisis with the Inca. Yielding to the persuasions of Pizarro, he had issued orders throughout his empire for the safe conduct of three soldiers, who were sent as emissaries to Cuzco for hastening the collection of the ransom.

It was a venturesome journey of more than six hundred miles, and as Pizarro did not care to risk the lives of his cavaliers in such an enterprise, he despatched three common soldiers from the ranks. They were entirely unknown, these base-born freebooters, and, unaccustomed to receiving such attentions as the abject Peruvians heaped upon them, became insolent and haughty, on the road and in Cuzco, the capital, giving rein to the worst passions of their depraved natures. They were carried all the way on the shoulders of natives, served at the inns and nobles' palaces with the best the land afforded, and treated, indeed, as though they were royalty itself, instead of merely members of a marauding band that had secured temporary possession of the country's sovereign.

But, though they disgusted and enraged all classes by their behavior, in Cuzco even daring to violate the vestal virgins' sanctuary, they were deferred to, on account of the Inca's peremptory commands, and given all the gold in the temple for transmission to Cassamarca. The stories they had to tell almost surpassed belief, but they showed seven hundred plates of gold, stripped from the walls of the sun's great temple, and pointed to two hundred Indian porters laden with the golden spoils.

XIII

THE INCA AND HIS MURDERERS

1533

WHAT a day was that in Cassamarca, when the emissaries returned from Cuzco! It was filled with rejoicings, and the Inca was as delighted as the soldiers of Pizarro at the successful outcome of their hazardous journey. He may have felt some pangs of regret when the adornments of the temple were exposed to view: those plates and bars of gold which had been lavished by his ancestors upon the abode of their deity. But were they not the price of his freedom?

The great room was now filling rapidly, with such a variety of golden plate, tiles, goblets, salvers, vases, such ingenious creations of the barbaric artisans, that the Spaniards gasped in wonder and astonishment. All were beautiful – too beautiful to go to the melting-pot – but among them were several objects that claimed particular attention. One of these was a golden fountain, of which not only the basin and sparkling jet of water were imitated, but, as well, aquatic birds that played about them and disported in the spray. Another was a sheaf of maize, with ear of solid gold incased in leaves of silver, and golden tassel pendent. If any object in nature were worth imitating it surely should be the maize, or Indian-corn, which for centuries had fed the natives of America, and was destined to prove such a blessing to countless thousands in both worlds divided by the great waters. Some of these inestimable treasures of art were preserved, for exhibition in Spain; but the most of them were melted into ingots, in which shape they were more easily divided among the impatient conquerors.

Ever since the return of the emissaries from Cuzco, in fact, the soldiers had clamored for an immediate partition of the spoils, realizing the dangers in delay; but a full month was consumed in recasting and reckoning up the value of this treasure, so that by the time the day of division came round the soldiers were almost ready to tear one another into pieces for their shares. If Pizarro had wished to deprive any one of his portion, he surely did not dare, and the result was that all received what was due them, though many were far from satisfied.

The grand total amounted to more than fifteen million dollars, of which first the "King's fifth" was set aside, then Francisco Pizarro's share, which amounted to more than half a million (including his booty in silver). His brother, Hernando, received half as much as he, Hernando de Soto half the sum given to the former, and so on, in a descending scale, the cavalry receiving more than eight thousand golden pesos each, and the infantry four thousand.

Besides his share of the ingots, Pizarro appropriated the great golden throne in which the Inca had made his entry into the city, and which was valued at not less than two hundred thousand dollars. Then the recently erected church of San Francisco, the first in Cassamarca and in Peru, was remembered with an endowment of twenty-three thousand dollars, and the monks and clerigos were not forgotten. All this was done in the most solemn manner, after invoking the continued blessing of heaven upon the enterprise, and accompanied with legal formalities.

It was impossible that everybody should be content, however, and the disgust of some was so great that it nearly resulted in bloodshed. This discontent was chiefly manifested by a body of men that had joined Pizarro after the capture of Atahuallpa had been effected, but before the spoils had been divided. It was two hundred strong, and in point of fact outnumbered the original conquerors, so that, in case of a trial of strength, it might have gone hard with the latter.

This company was commanded by Diego de Almagro, who (the reader will recall) had been the stanch supporter of Pizarro, and was entitled by contract, solemnly signed and witnessed, to one-third of whatever spoils he might acquire. The good clerigo, Luque, was also entitled to a third; but he had passed to his final account, and so had forfeited his share; while here was Almagro, the one-eyed partner of Pizarro, demanding an accounting.

He had faithfully performed his duties, inasmuch as he had raised two hundred men, fifty of whom were cavalry, and in three ships had sailed from Panama for Peru. After prolonged search, he had come upon the trail of Pizarro, and followed it from Tumbez to San Miguel. In that settlement he was cautioned against trusting himself in the power of his partner, to whom his own secretary sent warning that Almagro had come with the purpose of establishing an independent government. But the magical lure of gold was sufficient to lead him on, and his confidence in his own strength supreme, so he started for Cassamarca, which he reached in February, 1533.

When the old partners met they fell into each other's arms and embraced like brothers; and when Pizarro was told by Almagro that he had hanged his secretary to a tree, on learning of his treachery, the former was moved to tears. He did not offer, however, to divide his newly acquired wealth with Almagro – though that would have been in accord with their agreement – nor could he be persuaded to do so.

He lamented the death of the faithful Luque, who had been the life and soul of the enterprise, and but for whom it might have failed, but in his heart rejoiced that one the less was left to reckon with. With the remaining one, Almagro, he compounded for one hundred thousand pesos, giving to his soldiers the absurdly small sum of twenty thousand more, or about one hundred pesos apiece. How small it was may be seen by comparing the amount with some of the prices current in the camp for things in common use. A head of garlic cost half a peso; a bottle of wine cost seventy, and a horse fifteen hundred pesos, such was the enhancement of prices consequent upon the great abundance of gold in Cassamarca; while (according to Oviedo, the historian) "creditors shunned their debtors, and actually hid themselves, to avoid being paid!"

However dissatisfied the soldiers of Almagro may have been (and they were not slow in expressing their discontent), they were finally pacified by the promise of more, and perhaps greater, spoil for the future, in which they would undoubtedly share. They could not expect, of course, to receive the winnings of a game they did not play; but henceforth they would be entitled to the same shares as the first arrivals.

What they had seen, Pizarro assured them, was only a specimen nugget, so to speak, of the country's vast resources. They had barely entered the country, had not even scratched the soil with a pick, or sunk a shaft; yet more than fifteen millions in gold had been obtained, while the true source of it was still unknown to them. All this, moreover, had come mainly from a single city, Cuzco, which was six hundred miles away, and still unvisited, save by those three unarmed soldiers, who did not bring off a tithe of its treasures. Almagro's soldiers listened, and for a time were silenced, placated by promises; but they joined with Pizarro's impatient cohorts in a deafening cry of "On to Cuzco!"

Pizarro allowed himself to be swayed by the vociferous clamor of his men, and consented to lead the advance upon the capital so soon as he should consider it safe. But, as the commander-in-chief of the enterprise, and responsible for any disaster to the men in his charge, he refused to be driven to that step before he was ready. To cut loose from his base of supplies, and leave the Inca at large, with power to collect an army to oppose him, seemed the height of folly, as it undoubtedly was.

What, then, should he do? Atahuallpa was already demanding his release, declaring that he had complied with the conditions, by furnishing, if not a room-full of treasure, at least approximately that. Had it not been for the impatience of the Spaniards themselves, he said, the full amount would have been forthcoming; but their rapacity defeated his object by frightening the priests and custodians of the temples, who secreted much that would otherwise have been obtainable. Pizarro recognized the justice of this assertion, and caused to be issued a proclamation, drawn up by a notary, to the effect that the Inca had paid his ransom in full, and hence was entitled to his freedom; but, owing to the critical situation of the Spaniards – a mere handful of men surrounded by myriads of natives, who still owed allegiance to the deposed ruler – it would not be politic to release him at that time.

This was the first act in the proceedings by which Atahuallpa lost his life; the second was forced upon Pizarro mainly by Almagro's men, who were hungering and thirsting for spoils, and who saw no opportunity for gratifying their desires while the Inca remained alive. So they shouted: "Kill him! kill him! Make way with the wretch, and lead us to the capital!" They threatened, indeed, to march upon Cuzco as an independent command, and Pizarro knew well enough that their captain, Almagro, would be more than willing to lead.

In his desire to keep his men together and maintain his authority, he finally yielded to their demands and ordered Atahuallpa brought to trial.

The question naturally arises: On what charges could he be tried? The truthful answer would be, that there were no charges which his accusers could prove. The first article in his indictment was that he had caused the death of his defeated rival and half-brother, Huascar Inca. This unfortunate, and only legitimate, claimant to the Incarial throne had been kept a prisoner in Cuzco until shortly after the imprisonment of Atahuallpa.

One day it was revealed to the latter that Pizarro intended sending for Huascar and submitting the claims of the two to arbitration. This proposal was not relished by Atahuallpa, who is said to have sent secret orders to Cuzco, as the result of which Huascar was taken from prison and, in charge of a guard, sent forward on the road to Cassamarca. Somewhere on the way he was strangled and thrown into a river; and that was the last ever heard from Huascar Inca, except that messengers arrived at Cassamarca, who had previously been despatched by him, urging Pizarro to free him from his chains, in reward for which he would be his faithful tributary and ally. He is said, also, to have been seen by the soldier-emissaries, when on the road to Cuzco, to whom he made a vain appeal, promising to double the ransom Atahuallpa had offered, as he alone knew everything respecting the treasures of the royal city.

It is probable that Atahuallpa caused the death of Huascar Inca, when he found that the results achieved by his hard-fought battles might be neutralized by the decision of Pizarro in favor of his rival. He had won the throne – and lost it; but he still hoped to regain it. If he could not, at least no other should sit there; he would be the last Inca of Peru!

The second count in the indictment was that he had incited a rising of his people, who had banded together, and were already marching in immense numbers to attack the Spaniards. They were then about a hundred miles distant, rumor said, at a place called Huamachuco. This rumor was believed by Pizarro, who caused the patrols to be doubled, ordered the cavalry to keep their horses always saddled, and all soldiers to sleep on their arms. At the same time, he sent his favorite lieutenant, Ferdinand de Soto, to reconnoitre with a troop, in the direction of Huamachuco, and when the hostile forces should be discovered to return at once and report. Atahuallpa viewed the departure of De Soto with deep misgivings, for the frank and honest cavalier had won his confidence. "Do not go," he said to him (though, according to some, it was to Hernando Pizarro), "for if you do, that fat man and that one-eyed man will surely have me killed." The "one-eyed man" was Almagro, from whom he certainly had much to fear; and the "fat man" was Riquelme, the king's treasurer, who had come up from San Miguel to spy upon Pizarro.

If Atahuallpa had said, "the fat man, the one-eyed man, and the rest" he might have been justified, for all, with few if any exceptions, were thirsting for his blood. They wanted to go on to Cuzco, but feared either to take the Inca with them, to leave him behind a prisoner, or to set him free. In the circumstances, of course, the only alternative was to *kill him* – and this they resolved to do. But it must be done "legally and in order." The conquistadores had a justifiable horror of all lawyers, and many a time had memorialized the king not to allow any of those "pestiferous bachelors" to visit their colony; but they recognized the necessity for acting under legal forms. Oh yes! Atahuallpa was legally tried, legally condemned, and legally executed – according to the formal paper which was afterwards drawn up and sent to Charles, the king. He was allowed a counsel for defence, and on the bench sat, as judges, Pizarro and Almagro, neither of whom had he injured. On the contrary, he had conferred upon them benefits beyond measure.

Perhaps he might have been acquitted, as it was, if it had not been for the enmity of – first, the natives of Cassamarca province (who started the rumors of a rising instigated by the Inca), and of the interpreter, Felipillo, who was apprehended in an intrigue with one of Atahuallpa's favorite wives. The penalty of his transgression, had the Inca been in power, would have been death; but as Felipillo could claim that he was doing no worse than his masters, he escaped without punishment. [14]

But Atahuallpa had incurred the enmity of the interpreter by suggesting that he should be put to death, and as he was the only medium through which the Inca's answers to the charges could be obtained, he perverted them to suit his base purpose, and virtually wrought the ruin of the sovereign.

Atahuallpa was, in effect, condemned before he was tried, for Pizarro caused a chain to be put about his neck, and he was led like a felon to the dock. He was already doomed – that he knew – but he walked with firm step to the square, in which the court was held, and with unblanched cheek listened to the sentence quickly passed upon him. It was *death* – by burning at the stake, if he should still persist in his "idolatrous belief"; but by strangling, if he should, at the last moment, "consent to become a Christian!"

Again was the centre of the plaza the scene of murder most foul, when, at the close of that very day on which sentence had been passed, the Inca was conducted to the execution-place. He walked without support, his head erect, and with the dignity of a sovereign. He had made his protest – a last appeal to Pizarro – when doomed to die; now he was silent. Chained hand and foot, he was bound to a stake, fagots were piled around him to his waist, and the executioner but awaited the signal to set them on fire.

The shades of night had fallen and the plaza was enveloped in gloom, pierced only by the light of torches held in the hands of grim soldiers, who, in double ranks, encircled the place of execution. The moment had arrived when Atahuallpa was about to suffer the extreme penalty, as proclaimed by sound of trumpet, in the great square, where he had been wont to resort for festive ceremonies. Outside the circle of light shed by the flickering torches, all was dark and silent – silent, save for the sound of lamentation, wrung from hearts bursting with anguish. There was gathered the household of the Inca, there stood his retainers, a sad and somber group, helpless to save their sovereign.

The Inca raised his head and looked around, seeking in vain a look of sympathy. A sigh escaped him then, for the great Atahuallpa, at whose mere nod thousands once had trembled, was now alone, indeed, without a friend.

Suddenly the enclosing circle opened and towards the doomed one strode the Dominican monk, Valverde. In one uplifted hand he held a cross, in the other the book which Atahuallpa once had spurned. Since then, at intervals during his imprisonment, the monk had labored with him "for the good of his soul," as he expressed it. Now he once more proffered him an opportunity – the last – to renounce his idolatrous belief and embrace the religion of his enemies.

"Renounce, or you shall be burned," said the monk. "Become like one of us, and you will be strangled merely. O man of sin, will you not look upon this cross and become a Christian?"

The Inca had looked at him with dull eyes, perhaps unseeing; yet, it is said, he bowed his head, as a sign that he accepted the dread alternative – but more probably it fell from weakness.

The monk turned eagerly to the soldiers. "He has recanted! He dies a Christian!" he cried; and then he baptized his bewildered convert in the name of "Juan de Atahuallpa."

It would seem that, having by this renunciation cut himself off from friends, kindred, and the religion of his ancestors, Atahuallpa was entitled to the poor gift of his life. But no! while the surrounding soldiers, including Almagro and Pizarro, received the announcement with delight, they made no motion to secure his release. They were still determined upon his death, and remained passive, while the executioner slowly strangled his victim with a cross-bow string, soothing their consciences by chanting the *credo*, or creed of the Church to which he now belonged. Such was their monstrous depravity, in fact, that they took great credit to themselves in allowing the Inca to be strangled, or garroted, instead of being burned at the stake!

The struggles of the royal victim soon were over. As the last convulsive shudder shot through his frame, and his head fell forward on his breast, a word of command rang out, the soldiers with their torches fell into line and marched to their quarters, leaving the last of the Incas where he died.

XIV

IN THE HEART OF PERU

1533

SURROUNDED by a guard, the body of the Inca remained overnight in the plaza, but in the morning was taken to the church the Spaniards had built and interred with pomp and ceremony. This tardy honor to the deceased, it was thought, would give great satisfaction to the nobles and caciques, since he was buried "as if he had been a Spaniard"; but the funeral rites, though solemn and impressive, were not so regarded by his people, who invaded the church in crowds, and filled the air with shrieks and lamentations.

They were forcibly expelled, and told that Atahuallpa no longer belonged to them, having died a Christian; but several of his wives and sisters (it is related) hastened to their quarters, and there committed suicide, in order to join their lord and master in the celestial abode to which they believed he had gone. They could not believe that he had, by a mere nod of his head, transferred his allegiance to the God of the strangers. They cherished his memory, notwithstanding his apostasy, and after the Spaniards had left Cassamarca some devoted followers secretly exhumed his remains and transferred them to Quito, the "City of the Kings."

The barbarity of this heinous act of Pizarro is apparent on the face of it, and needs no comment from the historian. While the capture and imprisonment of Atahuallpa may have seemed a military necessity, there was absolutely no excuse for the attendant massacre, and for the crime committed in putting the Inca to death. Had he been cast in the ordinary mould of humanity, Pizarro must have suffered from remorse, especially when, a few days after the execution, De Soto returned and reported that there was no hostile army, and that the rumor of a rising instigated by the Inca was absolutely false. The generous cavalier was wrought to a pitch of indignation almost beyond restraint. He strode into the presence of Pizarro and denounced the execrable deed in unmeasured terms.

Steeped in crime as he was, Pizarro had the sensibility to blush with shame, and sought to cast the blame upon Riquelme, the treasurer, and Valverde, the priest. They in turn recriminated, and through the squabble that ensued, when these murderers met face to face, it became evident to all that they had done to death an innocent man.

"You knew I was his friend," exclaimed De Soto, reproachfully, "and so sent me away that I might not be here to defend him! It was a dastardly crime, and, moreover, one committed without a precedent. You had no right to bring to trial one so high in station as the Inca. He was a *king*, and only the king, our emperor, should have sat in judgment on him!"

With this startling statement, De Soto turned on his heel and left the trio confounded. They had not, probably, thought of that. Atahuallpa had been made captive so easily, and had been so long a prisoner, on familiar terms with all, that they had lost sight of his kingly prerogatives. Yet, that he *was* a king, and as such entitled to the form of trial mentioned by De Soto, was now apparent to every one.

"We have made a great mistake," said Riquelme, with a shrug.

"Perhaps," replied the monk, "but we can gloss it over. It is, meseemeth, a small matter that we have shortened the Inca's mortal life by a few years, when in return we have snatched his soul from perdition! This will have weight with the emperor, and especially with St. Peter's vicar, the pontiff. Came we not here to save souls? Yea, verily!"

"That is the chief part of our mission," assented Pizarro, eagerly. "Never have I lost sight of that, good father, as you can testify. Gold we must have, but souls we must save. And, moreover, it is not too late to amend what we have done. We have deprived these people of their ruler, 'tis true; but there are others just as fit to rule. It is the *shadow of authority*, and not the man, these Peruvian cattle reverence. Now I bethink me, there is among the prisoners a young man, half-brother to Atahuallpa, who will suit our purpose well. It matters not whether the son of Huayna Capac by one concubine or by another sits the throne. I have unmade one Inca, and I can as easily make another. Ho there, Felipillo! hither."

Close upon Pizarro's command, the interpreter came in and stood cringingly before him.

"Boy, there is, I understand, a brother of Atahuallpa among the prisoners. Will he not make a good Inca, think you?"

"Yes, Señor Governor. As good as any other. The rightful heir, now that both Atahuallpa and Huascar are dead, is one Manco Capac. He is, in fact, the only legitimate heir, being a son of the great Huayna Capac by his own sister the queen. But he is far away, and this young man, Toparca –"

"He is here – that is enough – and he shall be crowned at once! Ho, Hernando, brother of my heart, assemble the cavaliers, bring out all the soldiers, for to-day we have a coronation! Cause the trumpet to sound, command that every one appear, as to a festive gathering, for we are to crown another Inca!"

Once again the great plaza filled with a tumultuous throng, assembled in all haste, and composed, not only of the various followers of Almagro and Pizarro, each with a grievance slumbering in his breast, but of the dark-browed Peruvians, dwelling gloomily upon the scenes of blood they had witnessed in that very square. The young Toparca, a slender, dark-eyed youth of seventeen, was brought from his cell and set upon the golden throne, which was placed in the centre of the square, on or near the spot where, but a few hours before, his brother had breathed his last.

He was filled with apprehension, and doubted not that, being so nearly related to the Inca, he had been selected to afford fresh sport for the conquerors. But he quailed not, nor, when Pizarro advanced with sword extended, did he withdraw his gaze from his ferocious visage, though vaguely wondering why it should be wreathed in smiles.

The sword descended, flatwise, upon his shoulders, and then Pizarro turned about and shouted, "Where's the borla? Did I not command that it should be brought here for this ceremony?"

The serried ranks around him moved uneasily, as a soldier stepped out, holding in one hand the fringed head-dress, badge of Peruvian royalty.

"Here it is," he said, in surly tone, and scowling at his commander. "But it is mine! Did I not snatch it myself from the brow of Atahuallpa?"

"Yes, yes," assented Pizarro. "Of a truth it is thine, my son; but lend it to me now, for without this trumpery around his head this puppet of mine will be no Inca to his people. Thou shalt have it again, after this ceremony is over." So saying, he took it from the soldier's hand and bound it round Toparca's brow.

For a moment the lad sat as if petrified; then, as he realized the significance of this act – that he, now, was a chosen "Child of the Sun" – he rose and made as though he would tear the scarlet fringe in fragments. But the eyes of Pizarro were on him, and again his sword was displayed, this time menacingly pointed at Toparca's breast.

"Down! down!" he growled, like a beast ravening his prey. "Sit you there and receive the homage of your people!"

With a deep sigh, the youth sank back upon the throne, and when the ranks had opened and let in the eager natives the air was rent with acclamations: "Long live the Inca, Child of the Sun, and his wife, the Moon! May he long dwell in the City of Kings ! May he dwell in the mansions of the sun, whither the good Atahuallpa has fled!"

Such were the cries that greeted the accession of young Toparca to the throne. He seemed to hear them not, but sat silent and distrait, though to the ears of Pizarro they were as welcome music.

"Ha!" he exclaimed, with satisfaction. "Did I not say that I could make as well as unmake? It is all the same to these two-legged llamas, so they have a shepherd called an Inca!"

It seemed, indeed, to make no difference to them whether the ruler's name were Toparca or Atahuallpa; but one thing Pizarro had overlooked: most of the warriors were from Quito, and hence the more inclined to acclaim a prince from their own province. Yet it was sad to reflect that Atahuallpa could so soon be forgotten!

Nothing now prevented the advance upon Cuzco, for every obstacle in the road had been swept aside. In the morning of a summer's day, 1533, the army set out on its long and fatiguing march, from first to last travelling over the magnificent highway that connected Cassamarca with the capital. Pizarro and Almagro led the advance in turn, for as yet there was no serious trouble between them, and accompanying the army were the new Inca and Chalcuchima, the old general captured by Hernando Pizarro. They were borne in litters on the shoulders of the natives, and surrounded by attendants in gay attire, who vied with one another to do them honor.

That the country was in a state of disturbance was manifested by the broken bridges, by a village in flames at times, and the ravaged condition of the fields. But the Spaniards encountered no opposition until they had arrived at the vale of Xauxa (pronounced Háwah), where the various bands of warriors which had hovered at a distance were consolidated into a single body of vast proportions. They were massed upon the opposite bank of a river which the Spaniards were obliged to cross. There was no bridge, and when the soldiers arrived at the river a cloud of missiles fell upon them; but, with Pizarro in the van, shouting "Santiago and at them!" they boldly plunged in and, swimming or wading, scrambled across.

There was little fighting after the river was forded, for the Peruvians dispersed in the mountains, and the Spaniards took possession of the beautiful hamlet of Xauxa, which was the place whence Hernando had enticed Chalcuchima. It was such a delectable spot that Pizarro resolved to rest there and refresh the main body of his army, meanwhile sending out sixty horsemen, in command of the valiant De Soto, to reconnoitre the route ahead, repair the bridges, and open communication with the great valley of the Apurimac.

It was on this reconnoissance that the Spaniards discovered the Peruvians could fight, and valiantly, when the odds were not overwhelmingly against them, for, as they reached the steep defile of a mountain, a torrent of warriors rolled down upon them and actually arrested their advance. Soldiers were slain by blows from ponderous battle-axes, horses were overturned by rocks rolled upon them, and brought to the ground by desperate Indians clinging to their legs, while the air resounded with the war-cries of the attacking enemy.

Led by De Soto on his powerful charger, the Spaniards pressed upward and onward, until at last they gained a level space on the mountain-top surrounded by dense forest. Here they remained for the night, with the Indians gathering round them like famished wolves, waiting only for dawn to break to sweep them into the deep gorges that yawned on every side. The night was passed in sleepless vigilance, the beleaguered soldiers expecting every moment to hear the onrush of Indian warriors; but between midnight and dawn, the silver notes of a bugle rang through the air. Up the steep stairways cut in the rocks, a reinforcement under Almagro was toiling in the darkness, determined to effect a rescue or perish. In short, the two commands were joined on the plateau, and when daylight had cleared the mists, it was found that the Indians had melted away and disappeared.

No further opposition was encountered on the march, and in due time, after a most toilsome journey, the valley containing Cuzco the capital was reached. But while the army was advancing, there occurred a death and a tragedy, both of which, combined, cast the deepest gloom over officers and soldiers. When Pizarro received word that a strong force of Peruvians had attacked and nearly overcome the pick of his troopers, he at once suspected Chalcuchima of secretly sending information to the enemy. When brought before him, the aged general denied the accusation, but to no avail. He was at once placed in chains, and told that when a junction had been effected with Almagro's forces he should be tried for his life by a court-martial.

This occurred at Xauxa, where shortly after – alarmed, perhaps, at the probable fate in store for himself – he youthful Inca drooped and died.

Greatly disturbed by this ill-omened happening to his plans, this also Pizarro charged to the account of Chalcuchima, and after the farce of a trial he was condemned to death by burning at the stake. This was the favorite form of punishment with the Spaniards when they wished to inflict the extreme penalty upon a prisoner; and ever around the pyre and its victim might have been seen flitting the cowled monk, Valverde. After Chalcuchima had been lashed to the stake, he approached, and, though he did not offer him the alternative he had proffered the Inca, solemnly warned him of what the hereafter held in store for all idolaters.

The aged warrior is said to have listened attentively, and to have replied, "The white men I do not understand, nor their religion." After that utterance he kept a stubborn silence, and did not break it even by a groan, as the cruel flames leaped up and ate into his quivering flesh. [15]

His eyes were raised as if to look in last appeal upon his supreme deity, the sun, and some of his followers, who were compelled to feed the flames that consumed their chief, whispered to one another that with his expiring breath he invoked the name of his god, Pachacamac.

XV

IN THE CITY OP THE SUN

1533-1534

LEAVING the treasure he had collected with a guard of forty men in Xauxa, Pizarro continued his march into the beautiful vale of Xaquixaguana (Hä-kee-ha-guánä), which, for its great natural charms, had been selected by many Peruvian nobles as a retreat, and where they had built attractive villas in the midst of delectable gardens. Here he was met one day by a young Peruvian, who promised to establish that control over the natives which had been lost when

Atahuallpa was executed. He was the one, indeed, in whom was vested the only right to the succession, for it was none other than Prince Manco Capac, a brother of the murdered Huascar, and legitimate son of the great Huayna Capac.

Then Pizarro rejoiced that fate had been so kind to him, in causing the deaths of Atahuallpa and Toparca, for thereby he was relieved of what, in the circumstances, might have been embarrassing burdens. For there was no doubt that the Indian prince, who came to him with a large retinue of nobles and escorted by a numerous army, was the only legitimate heir to the Incarial throne. He was a young man of engaging appearance, and blessed with intelligence far surpassing that of Atahuallpa – an intelligence, in truth, which was to cause the Spaniards trouble. It had been one of the charges against Atahuallpa that he had put all his relatives, descendants of the Incas, to death, not even stopping short of the most distant connections of the royal family; but the living presence of Prince Manco was in itself a refutation of that charge. Pizarro was delighted at the change wrought in the aspect of political affairs, and at once ranged the young Inca and his force beneath his banners. He assured him that his only mission in Peru was the punishment of his and the late Huascar's enemies, and to reduce the country to subjection under its lawful sovereign. To this end he had landed on its shores; in pursuance of this aim he had first captured, then, on proof of treason, condemned the Inca Atahuallpa, and, finally, he was then ready to assist Prince Manco with all the strength of his forces. This assertion, though the prince must have known it to be false, was borne out on the face of it, and made to appear true to the people by the combining of the two commands. Together they marched along, the soldiers and the Indians fraternizing like real brothers, and together they repelled an assault by a body of armed natives, who ambushed them in a defile of the mountains.

Emerging from the gloomy recesses of the sierras one afternoon, the Spaniards saw the city of Cuzco lying before them, its white towers gleaming in the slant rays of a setting sun. Then they knew their long journey was nearing its end, and that within their sight were the depositories of treasure which they had long desired to pillage. They could not reach it that night, however, and a camp was pitched in the valley outside the city walls. Strict watch was kept, for, notwithstanding the invaders had with them the only lawful claimant to the throne of the Incas, they knew that dissension and strife were rife in the land.

What their reception would be, they hardly dared to imagine; but this they knew: that, as opposed to the barbarian hosts, they might consider themselves invincible. They had reached the heart of the empire; they were about to look upon the great imperial city, and enjoy a privilege which had been denied the unfortunate Atahuallpa, who had halted too soon and too long on his journey thither from the distant city of Quito.

It was on the morning of November 15, 1533, exactly one year after their entry into Cassamarca, that the Spaniards approached the city gates of Cuzco, capital of Peru. For a twelvemonth they had planned and schemed to this end; for eight years and more the commander of that band of veterans had had in mind the consummation about to be realized. In battle array, with De Soto leading, at the head of his cavalry, Pizarro commanding the centre and one of his brothers the rear-guard, the troops made their entrance into the great square of Cuzco, which was surrounded, like the plaza of Cassamarca, with massive structures of stone. Their arms and accoutrements shone in the sun, their banners fluttered in the breeze, and their martial tramp woke the echoes of the ancient city.

They were prepared for whatever might occur, realizing their isolation, six hundred miles from any force that could come to their aid, in the heart of the enemies' country. But, though the natives thronged the broad streets by thousands, and jostled one another in their eagerness to view those fair and bearded "Children of the Sun," they made no hostile demonstration, and allowed the strangers to take possession of the plaza without protest. Here they pitched their tents; here they picketed their horses; and here, for weeks thereafter, they remained, pillaging the palaces and temples by day, and at night slumbering on their weapons. Rumors of their doings had preceded them, and the natives regarded the strangers as hardly less than immortal. Thus their prestige protected them from assault, and, coming in company with the rightful heir to the imperial crown, they received the homage of the people. By the side of grim Pizarro, mounted on his fiery steed, with a white plume in his helmet and a naked sword grasped in his strong right hand, Indian carriers bore young Manco Capac, in a palanquin adorned with a canopy and shining with gems. The acclaim of shouting thousands, which rolled along like the sound of sea-waves breaking on the shore, was for him, their sovereign in prospective; but for Pizarro and his men were their openmouthed admiration and wonder.

The Spaniards found the architecture of Cuzco to be similar to that of Cassamarca, though the former exceeded in the number of its beautiful buildings. Around the central plaza were the same barrack-like structures of stone, one story in height, with low, broad doorways, and scattered throughout the city were numerous large dwellings, the palaces of the nobles. Towering over all, perched on a crag jutting out from the hill-side, rose a tower-like fortress, with circling parapets so well constructed that they seemed hewn out of solid rock.

The long, straight streets, the square, and the causeway leading to it, were paved with small pebbles, while the canal-like stream that supplied the city with water was spanned by bridges of hewn stone. No grander city, nor one more profusely supplied with magnificent structures, could be found in Spain, says an ancient authority; while words fail in describing the splendor of the vast temple containing the great golden effigy of the sun. It stood in its grandeur like a stupendous cliff, its grim exterior conveying no hint of the unique beauty of its interior decorations. Its chief ornaments, the golden plates and tiles, had been removed by the orders of Atahuallpa, and had long since been transformed into ugly ingots, valuable only for their intrinsic worth; but there still remained that simulacrum of the sun, its radiant rays extending from roof to floor. Also, there remained the frieze or cornice of gold, set into the rock and running all around the ceiling, truly a part of the structure itself, and on this account difficult to remove.

Allowed to plunder at will, but on condition that private dwellings should be respected and all pillage deposited with the royal treasurer, the eager soldiery soon divested the temples and palaces of their adornments, in their reckless quest robbing corpses in their graves and desecrating many a tomb. In the public storehouses, also, they found rich treasure, consisting of golden utensils in great variety, bales of fine cloths, gold beads, and sandals. The most unique of spoils were found in a cavern outside the city, where were stored, among other rare works of the native artisans, four golden llamas and a dozen statues of life size, representing women, probably queens or princesses. These, together with the golden effigies of the Incas, shared the common fate, and were melted into ingots with the rest.

Including the plunder along the route, among which were ten planks of solid silver, twenty feet in length and a foot in breadth, the combined spoils, after having been melted into bars by the Indian goldsmiths, amounted to more than six million dollars. After the customary fifth had been deducted for the crown, and the Pizarros had rewarded themselves, as in the division of the spoils at Cassamarca, there remained an amount sufficient to bestow about seventy thousand dollars upon each of the horsemen, and half as much upon the foot-soldiers, so that every man in the army was made rich.

It can hardly be said that, though all were enriched in a day, they had obtained more than their deserts, for they had toiled incredibly hard, and at the moment were involved in perils from which they might never be able to extricate themselves. Could they have retired, each man with his portion, to their homes in distant Spain, they might have lived there in luxury during the remainder of their lives; but, aside from the obstacles in the way of such a course, nothing was further from their thoughts than to do so.

Every man in the army was wealthy, and every man was a gambler by instinct, so it was not long before an epidemic of gambling broke out and swept all before it. In a single day, or night, many a soldier was deprived of the gains which he had suffered so much to acquire. The expert gamblers were few, of course, while the victims were many, so it resulted that the more dishonest of the soldiers secured the spoils.

One of these misguided soldiers was ever after known as "the fool who gambled away the sun before sunrise." To him had fallen, as his share of spoils, the great golden sun that once shone in the temple, and which he lost at cards in a single night – hence the expression, which passed into a by-word in Peru.

As before, in Cassamarca, gold and silver were so abundant that the prices of other things rose correspondingly to their depression in value, and it soon came about that a pair of shoes cost thirty pesos, a sword fifty, and a cloak a hundred, while rich food and drinks were scarce at any price.

Pizarro had obtained possession of Cuzco, anciently the seat of Peruvian authority, without striking a single blow. He had occupied the city and its fortresses, pillaged its temples, and ransacked its palaces, without asking leave of a single individual. But, in order to give his acts the sanction of authority, he lost no time in proclaiming the succession of Manco Capac to the throne which he himself had stained with the blood of its former occupant.

At the coronation, which shortly ensued, all the olden ceremonies were revived, and the new Inca received the red-fringed borla from the hands of Pizarro himself. He received it from the conqueror – that was the humiliation of the act; he was surrounded by the mailed warriors of an alien people, and his accession was proclaimed by the trumpets of strangers.

Yet the servile Peruvians gave him glad acclaim, and received young Manco Capac as Inca in place of the one Pizarro had deposed and murdered. In his veins flowed the blood of great Huayna Capac, and it was a triumph of diplomacy on Pizarro's part to set up this sovereign – even if merely to overthrow him later. It then served his purpose to have an Inca in his hands whom he could control and through him the millions of people, who had been left without a head, when Pizarro lopped it off at Cassamarca.

Behold him, then, the supreme, yet powerless, Inca, seated at the right hand of his conqueror, upon an elevated platform in the plaza, where all can see and hear! From cups of gold they quaff each other's health, in draughts of foaming chicha, not forgetting to "toast" the royal mummies, which, having been brought from their sepulchres and ranged on seats about the festive board, were waited on by attentive servitors.

The people shout and dance and sing in honor of the reinstated house of Huayna Capac. In young Manco they see the old warrior personified, and in him hope for a renewal of the glories of the past regime. They look upon Pizarro as the war-lord of their Inca, come to fight his battles; but Manco himself is not deceived, neither are his war-chiefs, secreted in the mountains, with their soldiers by the thousand, in the guise of shepherds and cultivators!

He realizes his position; he knows that Pizarro is his master; but, the while the ceremonial banquet drags along, he whispers to himself, perhaps, "Wait and see." Atahuallpa lost his throne through an overweening confidence in his greatness, in his armies; he would commit no such mistake, for he knew more than Atahuallpa knew. He knew the Spaniards were for the moment invincible, while his own warriors were scattered, his armies disorganized; but he would play a game of duplicity and cunning, until the strangers, disarmed by his apparent submission, should have become weak by dissipation, their soldiers dispersed, and their munitions exhausted. Wait and see!

Meanwhile, deceived by the servile submission of the Inca, Pizarro devoted his energies to intrenching himself strongly in the capital. He organized a government, appointing *alcaldes* and *regidores*, among these last being two of his brothers, Juan and Gonzalo. We have not seen much of these brothers since they landed in Peru; but they have already done valiant service, for they were worthy of their distinguished kinsman, and soon were to rise to eminence themselves. Upon them and other captains were bestowed the palaces taken from native nobles, as well as their retinues of servants, while Francisco himself now took his military title of captain-general, and was henceforth addressed as "governor."

A noble cathedral was built, a nunnery was established in the house of the vestal virgins, and these "daughters of the sun" were thrust forth to fare as they might, the prey of the licentious soldiery. Among them were many who had been destined for the Inca's household – his wives, in fact; and the heart of Manco Capac swelled with grief and rage. But he was helpless, for Pizarro had grasped the substance of power, while he held only the shadow. He knew, however, that Cuzco was not all the empire, that it was but a golden grain in the sands of the sea. The vast territory of Peru, with its teeming millions, contained latent resources, in ferocious fighting-men which, once aroused, would, under his leadership, sweep the invaders from the face of the earth. Manco Capac did not doubt his capacity for leadership, but he had never tested his powers in open field; hence, when invited to accompany Almagro, in a campaign against a force of natives under Quizquiz, one of the generals who had won victories for Atahuallpa, he gladly consented to go. Quizquiz was overcome and killed, his army dispersed, and Manco Capac, having materially assisted Almagro, returned with him to Cuzco to receive the praises of Pizarro.

XVI

QUARRELS OF THE CONQUERORS

1534-1535

STRANGE as it may appear, Manco Capac had taken great pleasure in assisting at the defeat of Quizquiz, the valiant Peruvian, because most of his soldiers were men of Quito, to which city and province belonged a faction from which he had much to fear. Indeed, the men of Quito were invariably plotting treason in his camp, and intriguing against him. When, in the progress of events, Manco Capac could endure no longer the humiliations imposed upon him, and endeavored to escape to the mountains, warriors of Quito in the service of Pizarro betrayed him, and brought about his capture.

That episode of the conquest will be narrated in due course; meanwhile, let us turn to glance for a moment at that portion of olden Peru lying on and north of the equator, known as Quito. As [16] we have seen already, it was the birthplace of Atahuallpa, and during the latter years of Huayna Capac his chosen place of residence.

The unparalleled achievements of Pizarro in Peru had drawn to that country the attention of all the Spanish adventurers in America, as well as of those at home desirous of emulating their careers. Among others was that valiant but unscrupulous officer who served with Cortés in Mexico, Pedro de Alvarado. He was then governor of Guatemala, which country he had conquered, and was enjoying wealth and honors that should have satisfied the most towering of ambitions; but, casting his eye towards Peru, and noting that Quito had not been invaded, he resolved to conquer it. So he diverted from its original destination a fleet that had been intended for the Spice Islands, and with five hundred men, well equipped, landed on the southern coast. In short, he marched upon Quito, which he finally reached after terrible sufferings while crossing the Cordilleras; but was not permitted to taste the fruits of conquest, since he had aroused enemies far more formidable than the natives of the country. For Pizarro, on receiving the alarming rumors of this invasion of his territory, immediately despatched Almagro to intercept Alvarado, and, if possible, induce him to quit the territory.

Though he pressed forward with the utmost rapidity, Almagro found, on reaching San Miguel, that the commandant of that place, Sebastian Benalcazar, had anticipated his design, and himself hurried off to make the capture of Quito. Both commanders, in fact, reached and grasped the coveted prize before Alvarado arrived, and with united forces calmly awaited his coming. There was then the prospect of a bloody encounter, for the redoubtable hero of Guatemala and Mexico was the equal in valor and military training of any captain of his time. But, though he had a force vastly superior in numbers to his opponents, it had been weakened by starvation to such an extent that he hesitated to give battle.

In brief, negotiations were entered into which resulted in the fiery Alvarado agreeing to withdraw from the country for a consideration of one hundred thousand *pesos de oro*, or about a million dollars, which, he claimed, was less than his armament had cost him, not to mention the privations he had endured.

Thus the matter was settled amicably, and the two principals retired upon Pachacamac, where they met Pizarro, who cordially ratified the compact, and entertained Alvarado with banquets and tournaments. This meeting of the two great conquerors was a notable event. They were never to meet again, for Alvarado, who was known to the Mexicans as *Tonatiuh*, or (as the Inca was called) a "Child of the Sun," departed from the country soon after, and was killed by a fall from his horse in 1541, the same year in which Pizarro was assassinated.

Now that Pizarro had turned away Alvarado and absorbed the greater portion of his large army and armament; now that he and his captains had subjected to his rule the two extremes of the empire and the intervening country – all this accomplished, and the Inca his abject slave – he set himself to the founding of cities. In his capacity of founder, as promoter of peace and commerce, we shall see the warlike Pizarro in a new and more attractive role than hitherto. The stern and relentless conqueror was getting old, and though still filled with all the ardor of youth, as it seemed, he desired to settle down at peaceful avocations.

Seeking the most desirable site for a capital, he happily found it in the beautiful valley of Rimac, on a river which flowed into the Pacific, not far distant. Here, on January 6, 1535, he laid the first stones of the city known as Lima, which had a wonderful growth from the first, and is now numbered among the finest cities of South America. His army of soldiers he converted into an army of workmen, none of whom labored harder at the upbuilding of the city than Pizarro himself. But there was still another army, commanded by Almagro, who had gathered about him the best of Alvarado's soldiers, some of whom were "men of Mexico," who had fought and conquered with Cortés. Pizarro despatched Almagro to Cuzco, which he had left in charge of his brothers, to whom he wrote, confirming his old partner in the command of the city. Nothing was more to Almagro's liking than the governorship of Cuzco, though he still hoped, old as he was, to carry the conquest southward into Chile, on his own account, and never lost sight of that scheme. And now, while Francisco Pizarro is busy at the building of Lima, and Almagro watching over Cuzco as its governor, let us throw a glance across an intervening continent and ocean to Old Spain, where things are happening which will have an important influence upon subsequent doings in Peru. Soon after the Inca's treasure had been divided, at Cassamarca, Hernando Pizarro had been sent to Spain by his brother, in charge of the "king's fifth," and commissioned to secure all the honors he could for himself and his fellow-conquerors.

He arrived at Seville on a day in January, 1534, and at once proceeded to court, where he was received with open arms; for Charles V. was in need of gold at that time, and the sight of so much treasure opened his heart. He showed his pleasure by making Hernando a knight of Santiago, and bestowing upon Francisco the marquisate of Atavillos, besides confirming him in the governorship of all Peru. He also gave Hernando permission to recruit a force and equip an expedition, with the result that he returned to the isthmus with the largest fleet that had ever sailed to that region direct.

Many a Spanish cavalier was lured to his death by the tales told by Hernando respecting the vast wealth to be obtained in Peru, for few of the company sailing with him realized their hopes. Some died of starvation at Nombre de Dios, others perished in crossing the isthmus, and but a few reached the golden land, where they found that everything had been appropriated by the first arrivals.

Hernando himself was as the angel of death bearing to Peru the cause of a dissension worse than a pestilence. His return, in truth, marked the beginning of a feud which involved the sacrifice of hundreds of lives and the downfall of his family. It originated as follows: Besides the honors for himself and his brother, Hernando had secured from the king the bishopric of Cuzco for Valverde, the monk, and an independent governorship for Almagro. To Francisco Pizarro was assigned the territory of Peru, from a point a little north of the equator to another two hundred and seventy leagues south, beyond which Almagro was authorized to explore, to conquer, and to rule.

It was thought that by this apportionment the differences between the two chief conquerors might be satisfactorily settled; but at once, when the news arrived, arose the difficulty of running the dividing-line. No accurate survey could be made then, and, as both parties to this affair desired to hold the great city of Cuzco, both naturally insisted that it was within their jurisdiction. By one side it was held that Pizarro's southern boundary went beyond Cuzco, and by the other that it not only fell short, but barely included his new city of Lima!

It might have seemed as if Hernando had been very generous to Almagro, in securing him any concessions whatever, had it not been that the latter had sent with him an emissary of his own, who saw to it that Pizarro's former partner got his due. Hernando could not have done less, in the circumstances; and, on the whole, he doubtless considered it a very good arrangement, by which Almagro could be sent southward into Chile, where he might get lost, or be killed by the Indians. At all events, he would be out of the way. The contingency of a mutual claim to Cuzco he had anticipated by having his brother's southern boundary extended seventy leagues, so that there could be, he believed, no shadow of doubt on his title.

But old Almagro was obstinate. He had suffered much from the Pizarros: he had endured their contempt and revilings, had accepted but a meagre portion of the spoils, when by the terms of his contract with Francisco he was entitled to a moiety. Now that he was independent, however, and intrenched at Cuzco with a valiant following, he set the Pizarros at defiance.

Juan and Gonzales had delivered up the city to Almagro by Francisco's order; but close on the heels of the messenger who had brought it came a command for them to regain and hold it till the boundary-line had been adjusted, or at least the king's wishes on the subject known.

Sturdy old Almagro refused to yield an inch of territory or a single street of the city, and a fierce dispute resulted, to end which the governor hastened from Lima, where he was peacefully resting, and at once threw himself into the breach. Whenever these two – Pizarro and Almagro – came together, the latter always yielded to the former, who, indeed, ruled all men with whom he came in contact. So they embraced, and at once patched up a truce. In the end, Almagro consented to abandon Cuzco to the Pizarros and at once set forth on his expedition into Chile. They renewed their compact in the presence of a priest, calling upon the Almighty to witness that they invoked His wrath if either should violate the contract, or if either should do harm to the other. Eternal perdition was to be the share of him who broke it so far as they could invoke the torments of the world to come, and loss of life and property in this as was attested by a notary and a number of witnesses on June 12, 1535.

Having satisfied Almagro by another oath – the third or fourth they had mutually taken – t Pizarro sent him off to the southward, whither he went with a large and well-appointed army, accompanied by Manco Capac's brother and the high-priest, Villaoma, as guides and counsellors. Owing to his popularity, resulting from his generous disposition, Almagro had no lack of offers of service from the cavaliers, including among them, it is said, so renowned a *caballero* as Fernando de Soto, who aspired to be lieutenant-general of the command.

Having rid himself of his troublesome friend, Pizarro returned to the coast, leaving his two brothers, Juan and Gonzalo, in charge of Cuzco, and eagerly resuming his interrupted labors in Lima, which he called the "City of the Kings."

XVII

THE INCA RAISES HIS STANDARD

1535-1536

PIZARRO now had wealth beyond any expectation in which he had ever indulged; he had honors, also, greater than any his proud father had enjoyed; for, as Marquis of Atavillos, he had been admitted to the aristocracy of Spain. Such an elevation, of one who in youth had been a swineherd, might have turned the head of Francisco Pizarro if it had come to him at a previous period of his life; but he was now old enough to measure his honors by the proper standard. He had received no more than he merited, and, aside from the vast wealth he had won, his rewards were, in truth, hardly adequate for the thirty long years of persistent endeavor. Of one thing he was convinced: that he had had enough of fighting, and now desired only to spend his last years, if not in retirement, at least in peace.

The founding of cities and the promotion of agriculture were now more congenial to his temperament than the wielding of the sword. But he was not to be allowed to rest, for, after having, as he thought, conquered and pacified the country, he was suddenly called upon to gird himself again for battle, and thereafter was in constant turmoil. The cause of his next anxiety was the young Inca, Manco Capac, whom he had left virtually a captive in charge of Juan and Gonzalo Pizarro. We have seen that he had never abandoned the idea of assuming the authority which had been denied him, and was merely awaiting the right moment for striking a blow for liberty.

The dissensions of the Spaniards seemed to offer him this opportunity, and he promptly availed himself of it, as soon as the two great leaders, Pizarro and Almagro, had turned their backs upon Cuzco. Soon after Almagro's departure, the Peruvian high-priest, Villaoma, stealthily returned to Cuzco and held a long interview with the Inca. Hernando Pizarro was in command at the time, having superseded his brothers because of his superior ability. Though cruel and tyrannical, he had, somehow, won the sympathy of the Indians, who recalled that Atahuallpa had said, just before his death, that if Hernando had been in Cassamarca he would not have suffered so cruel a fate.

It is believed he was more lenient to the Inca than his brothers, and when Manco asked permission to retire for a few days into the country, in order to offer his annual tribute at the tomb of his father, he readily consented. His avarice may have been more potent, however, than his friendliness in securing the desired permission, as the crafty Indian had promised him a golden statue, which, he said, was concealed in a cave near his father's tomb. When the time had expired, at the end of which Manco was to return, Hernando's suspicions became aroused, and he sent out his brother, Juan, with sixty horsemen, to search for and bring back the recreant Inca. Meanwhile, what was occurring in the secluded mountain valley where the great Huayna Capac was buried? Had the Spaniards been able to penetrate the wall of rocks which hid it from their sight, they might have witnessed a sight that would have struck them with surprise, if not with terror, for there were gathered the chieftains of a hundred bands, and their followers to the number of at least a hundred thousand.

Standing by the tomb of the king were the Inca and his high-priest, the former lifted upon the shoulders of his subjects, the latter haranguing the Indians in a voice that penetrated far into the surrounding forest. "The time has come," he shrieked, "in which we are to avenge the thousands upon thousands of insults which have been heaped upon us! The time has passed for many of our nobles, who have been cut down; for our Inca, Atahuallpa, who was murdered; for our vestal virgins, who have been more than murdered. For them there is no redress. But for us who live, for your families, your wives, and sons, and daughters, there is yet hope of revenge! Here are vessels of chicha, the wine of our country; here in the presence of our Inca, lord and master, let him come and drink who this day resolves to fight until death for the rescue of our country!" Instantly there was great commotion. Spears tipped with gold and silver, pole and battle-axes edged with copper, were thrust by the thousand towards the brightly shining sun, as, with a mighty voice like the roar of mountain winds, the assembled warriors shouted: "Death to the strangers! Death to the murderers! Death to the violaters of our temples!"

The Inca was the first to drink, holding a golden goblet to his lips, and then exclaiming: "This is a pledge that we shall kill them all – all, and leave not one alive!" Then, as his warriors crowded eagerly around, he descended from his palanquin, and mounting a horse which had been kept in waiting till this moment, placed himself at their head.

"Henceforth," he said," your Inca leads; no longer will he follow! For this is our last hope. Unless we fight as those strangers fight, we cannot overcome them. Adopt their methods, turn their own weapons against them: thus we shall benefit by our sore experience."

This meeting was but the sequence to a series of drills, and of numerous secret assemblages during many months, by which the wild warriors had brought to their aid the military tactics of the Spaniards. Supplementing these with their natural liking for war, with their ferocity in combat, their disregard for life, their superior numbers, and craving for bloodshed, who could overcome them now? They lacked but the weapons of the strangers to make them every way their equals.

Led by Juan Pizarro, not the least courageous of the Pizarro brothers, to all of whom fear was utterly unknown, the sixty horsemen sent out by Hernando galloped across the plain and finally arrived at the river Yucay, where, on the opposite bank, they saw an Indian host drawn up in solid battalions. Shouting their battle-cry, the Spaniards dashed across the river and into the serried masses, committing great slaughter; but, though the foe retreated, they did so in good order, and when evening came it found the attacking party at a disadvantage.

Scarcely an eye was closed in sleep that night, and dawn revealed the forest swarming with the enemy. Great rocks came tumbling down upon the cavalry, and the air was filled with arrows, darts, and javelins, so that, while the Spaniards stubbornly refused to retreat, neither could they advance in the face of that terrible tempest. They held their position during that day and part of the next, when, greatly to the disgust and surprise of Juan Pizarro, an imperative order came from Hernando to retire upon Cuzco at once, as the city was invested by a multitude of warriors. Under a less careful commander, the retreat of the Spaniards might have become a rout, as the triumphant Inca and his horde pressed them so closely that they could scarcely save their wounded, and left their numerous dead on the field. Arrived within sight of the city, what was their astonishment to behold a vast host surrounding it on every side, through which it would have been impossible to cleave their way, had not the battalions about the gateway opened of their own accord, as though disdaining to combat so small a body of soldiers, when the entire army was destined to become their prey!

The brothers embraced, and hastened to the watch-tower on the crag, whence they could view the city, which seemed to be enclosed within a sea of human beings, from whose throats issued terrific shouts of rage and war-cries in a deafening chorus, which, added to the crash of drum and trumpet, created a veritable pandemonium.

When the sun had sunk behind the hills, and darkness covered the scene, the sky was crossed by trains of light, like shooting-stars, proceeding from hundreds of burning arrows, [17] which, descending upon the dry thatched roofs of palace and hut alike, soon caused the city to be wrapped in flames.

The two hundred Spaniards, together with their allies, numbering about a thousand, were entirely surrounded by fire, while dense volumes of smoke filled the air to suffocation. Fire and famine were the aids upon which the Peruvians relied to exterminate their enemies, but they never for a moment relaxed their individual efforts. When, at last, after enduring for three days the heat of this fiery furnace, some of the cavalry ventured forth, they were savagely attacked by Indians armed with lassos, who threw the horses to the ground and exultingly dragged their riders away to be killed at their leisure.

The desperate Spaniards made many sallies from the square, in which they were encircled by the flames, and committed great slaughter, but all to no purpose, the number of the Indians was so large.

Early in the siege, the Peruvians had gained possession of the fortress overlooking the city, from this post of vantage discharging torrents of missile weapons, and one day tossing thence several human heads, which the sorrowing Spaniards recognized as those of former companions who had settled in the country. This showed that the uprising was wide-spread, probably comprehending the whole country, and, as the Indians held all the mountain passes, a retreat to the coast was entirely out of the question. What had become of the governor, the beleaguered Spaniards often asked, as the weary days went by; but they well knew that he could not come to their rescue.

At last the fire from the fort became so annoying that Hernando resolved upon its capture. He detailed fifty men for this forlorn hope, whom he placed in charge of Juan Pizarro. Led by this gallant cavalier, they dashed up the heights, scaled the first of the circling parapets, and were attacking the second, when the Indians swarmed upon them in such numbers that they were overcome.

The intrepid Juan had been wounded the previous day, and in consequence had not worn his helmet, as it chafed the wound. While he was in the thick of the battle in front of the second parapet, a great stone descended with terrific force upon his unprotected head and brought him to earth. He attempted to rise, but was unable to, and his sorrowing companions gathered him in their arms and made the best retreat they could. Juan lingered a few days in agony, and then expired, the first of the brothers to die a violent death – but not the last!

Meanwhile, the Indians still held the fortress, and by their taunts and showers of missiles so enraged Hernando that he determined to take it, come what might. Even while poor Juan lay dying, he committed the defence of the city to Gonzalo, and himself led the attack upon the walls above. Scaling-ladders were placed against them, and up the Spaniards climbed, but only to be hurled headlong to the rocks below. Again and again these desperate men repeated their efforts, until finally they prevailed, and with yells of exultation leaped into the midst of the Indians. But few of the brave defenders were alive when this occurred; but one of them, a man of powerful build, said by some to have been the high-priest, Villaoma, was equal to a host of warriors. He wielded a ponderous battle-axe with such force that many a Spaniard went down before him. At last, charging upon him in a body, they drove him to the capstones of the parapet, where, for a moment, he poised himself defiantly, then, hurling his battle-axe into their midst, leaped out into space, and was dashed to pieces at the foot of the battlements. All the remaining Indians were put to the sword, and thus, at terrible loss of life, the fortress was won.

Holding now the key to the city, the Spaniards were enabled to keep the Peruvians in check; but they could not appear outside the blackened walls without being set upon by maddened thousands thirsting for their blood. For weeks and months the siege was protracted, and, all the provisions in the Inca's granaries having been exhausted, the besieged finally were compelled to endure the horrors of a famine. They made many a foray into the surrounding hills, sometimes returning with scanty supplies of provisions, but only obtained at the expense of valuable lives.

Leaving these heroic brothers of the governor for a while, let us seek information respecting the real hero of this narrative, Francisco. We have devoted some space to detailing their experiences, because they were within striking distance of the Inca's arm, and bore the brunt of the contest. But, while Cuzco, the ancient Peruvian capital, was the main object of attack, the insurrection had been universal, and the garrisons at Xauxa and Lima were not spared.

A large body of warriors made an assault upon Lima, but, not being under the immediate direction of the Inca, they were soon routed by Pizarro's cavalry, and chased across the plains into the mountains. Having secured himself and the city, Pizarro's next care was the relief of his beleaguered soldiers at Cuzco. He sent forward, at various times, four detachments of a hundred each, comprised of tried veterans and led by efficient officers; but they could not penetrate the mighty barrier of mountains that intervened between the valleys of Lima and Cuzco. All were cut off and ambuscaded by the swarming Indians, who rolled down great rocks upon the heads of the soldiers with fatal effect, and in the resulting confusion slaughtered them almost at will.

A few stragglers only returned to Lima, where the consternation of the people was such that they implored Pizarro to abandon the country and seek refuge on shipboard. But the stern old warrior spurned such cowardly counsel. He was never known to abandon a comrade to his fate, no matter what the odds against him. Moreover, he realized that the empire was at stake; and he knew the temper of his brothers at Cuzco: they would never surrender, so long as a man was left alive or an arquebuse fit to be fired.

And in the end his implicit trust in his comrades won the day. Instead of allowing the ships on the coast to be used for the purpose suggested by the craven populace, he despatched them all in search of succor. He wrote urgent letters to his friends in Panama, in Guatemala, and in Mexico, begging them, in the name of their king, and as Christians engaged in a common cause against the heathen, to hasten to his assistance before he and all his friends should be swept into the sea. He even wrote to Alvarado, so recently his enemy, to send him ships, with men and munitions, so that, as Spaniards, they could save and hold the empire he had all but won.

Six long and weary months dragged by, during which the Inca's troops held the Spaniards prisoners within the few fortified places in which they had taken refuge. The mountains were their strongholds, but on the plains they were no match for the cavalry, which cut them down and slaughtered hecatombs of their warriors.

At last, about midsummer, the Inca felt compelled to withdraw the bulk of his army from about Cuzco, in order to cultivate the neglected fields and prevent a threatened famine. The instinct of prudence, inherited from his ancestors, was strong within him; but by yielding to it he, in effect, signed the death-warrant of himself and his people. For, no sooner had he retired to the mountains, than Hernando sallied forth with all his available cavalry and ravaged the country, returning to Cuzco with thousands of llamas and vast quantities of grain. Then, refreshed by this sustenance so providentially supplied, the Spaniards grew aggressive, and deliberately slaughtered, not only such warriors as they could find, but all the women and children who came to their camps to serve them.

Learning that the Inca had taken refuge in a strongly fortified camp on a mountain-top, Hernando himself went in pursuit of him, hoping by his capture to put an end to the war. But, becoming entangled in a gloomy defile beneath the fort, he was set upon by the Inca's warriors in such numbers, that of the eighty horsemen with him, very few escaped the avalanche of rocks and hurricane of missiles launched upon them. From the ramparts above, Manco Capac peered down upon his discomfited enemy, and directed the assault, as well as the continued attacks upon the Spanish rear, when, finally overcome through sheer force of numbers, Hernando's horsemen withdrew in confusion and fled for the city, closely pursued by the victorious Peruvians.

This was the Inca's last victory, but not his last stand against his relentless foe. Driven farther and farther into the mountain wilderness, but ever maintaining his high courage and attitude of implacable hostility to the Spaniards, he gradually passed from sight, and was finally killed by some renegade soldiers, who, in return, were massacred by his incensed warriors.

XVIII

THE DOWNFALL OF ALMAGRO

1537-1538

THOUGH Hernando Pizarro had driven the enemy from Cuzco and its immediate neighborhood, he dared not send even a courier to the coast for tidings of his brother, as the mountains were still infested with roving bands of Indians. By putting some of his captives to the torture, he extorted from them the unwelcome information that the governor had abandoned Lima and had sailed for

Panama with all his people. They also said that the Inca had in his possession the skins of one hundred and fifty horses, the remains of Pizarro 's cavalry, and the heads of two hundred Spaniards slain in battle!

This dismal news convinced Hernando that he was left alone in the land with his decimated band; but he did not give over pursuit and persecution of the natives, nevertheless. While engaged in that occupation so congenial to his cruel nature one day, rumors reached him of the near approach to Cuzco of Almagro's army. For a while he was uncertain whether the "men of Chile" – as they were henceforth called – came as friends or enemies; but he was not left long in doubt. Soon an embassy arrived from Almagro, who sent a copy of his credentials from the crown, confirming him as marshal and adelantado, with a peremptory demand that he be given possession of the city.

That doughty commander had been defeated in his projected conquest of the great southern country – not by hostile armies, but by the elements. The asperities of nature had proved too great for him to overcome, especially with that loadstone at Cuzco pulling him back. He and his men had advanced hopefully and cheerily at first, but when at last they began to suffer from cold and hunger, when many had lost toes and fingers from frost-bites, and the provisions gave out, they resolved to return. The decision was not made, however, until the sufferings of the army had become acute, until the frozen carcasses of all their horses had been devoured, in the extremity of hunger, and there seemed actually no hope of reaching the land of gold – still far off beyond the snowy mountains. They had marched three hundred miles beyond the southern frontier of Peru before they set their faces northward again, on the return journey crossing a vast and dreary desert, and enduring great privations.

They were at Arequipa, less than two hundred miles from Cuzco, when they first heard of the Indian insurrection. They learned, also, that the Inca was still intrenched in his stronghold, not far from Cuzco. Though his force of nearly five hundred men far exceeded that of Hernando Pizarro, depleted as it was by the protracted contest, Almagro thought it might be desirable to secure Manco Capac as an ally, so sent to him, soliciting an interview. The Inca consented; but he had heard of the cruelties practised by Almagro upon the Indians of the south: of the chain gangs he had made up of the natives, compelling them to serve as beasts of burden until they dropped dead from fatigue; of the thirty Indian chiefs he had burned alive in revenge for the killing of three of his men. He was wary, therefore, and, convinced that no Spaniard could be trusted, when Almagro arrived at the place of rendezvous, in the vale of Yucay, set upon him with fifteen thousand warriors. He was defeated, driven back to his lair in the mountains, and Almagro no longer looked to him for help in the approaching contest with his own countrymen, but advanced against Cuzco with his veterans.

Two battles were fought for the possession of Cuzco, the first being a battle of wits, in which Hernando Pizarro won, with the aid of the city council, who brought about a truce; the second resulting from an attack in force by Almagro, when he found that, availing himself of the armistice, his enemy was placing the city in a posture of defence. At the same time, he learned, an army under Alonzo de Alvarado was marching up from the coast, which, if time were allowed, would surround and in all probability force him to surrender. There was need for haste, and thus it was that, one black and rainy night in April, 1537, the "men of Chile" dashed across the bridges into Cuzco, shouting lustily: "*El Rey y Almagro!*" – the King and Almagro – and all the time keeping up a smart fusillade with their muskets.

They captured the church and the square, then attacked the palace in which Hernando was lodged. This cavalier, though taken by surprise, inasmuch as several men of his guard were killed before he could put on his armor, made such an obstinate defence that, in order to compel him to surrender, the thatched roof was fired over his head. He stood the soldiers off for a while with his good Toledo blade, and was ably seconded by his brother, Gonzalo; but the flames finally drove them out, and they surrendered their swords as the blazing rafters fell around them with a crash. They were hurried off to a dungeon, and Almagro took formal possession of the city he and his followers had so long coveted, and to which they had often turned with longing when on the weary march into Chile.

Many of Pizarro's men went over to Almagro, and the proximity of Alvarado's force was indicated by numerous deserters, who informed the marshal that their commander was less than forty miles away, and marching rapidly upon the capital. Leaving a garrison in the fortress, Almagro hastened off to meet the new enemy, and thus for a while was between two fires, as it were – Hernando's sullen soldiers in Cuzco and Alvarado's advancing force in the mountains. But he went off gayly (for he was never so happy as when all his powers were called into action), and is said to have boasted that he would not leave one of those Pizarros to stumble over. This was a pun on the word *pizarra*, a slate or stone in the road, which he would kick out of his way with contempt. As he was setting out, his right-hand man, Captain Orgoñez, said to him: "Señor Mariscal, are you going to leave those Pizarros behind?"

"Why, to be sure," answered Almagro; "we cannot take them with us, you know."

"No, nor would I advise you to, Mariscal," answered Orgoñez; "but your life will not be worth a maravedi while they live, and" – drawing his hand significantly across his throat – "as our Spanish proverb hath it, 'only the dead man cannot bite'."

"Oho! they will not bite, for I shall draw their teeth," said the marshal, laughingly; "but kill them? No, not yet. Their brother is my partner, and I hope yet to force him to do me justice."

"Never!" exclaimed Orgoñez. "By what you have done to his brothers, he has received a deadly insult. A Pizarro never forgets – unless you cut off his head!"

Almagro had occasion to remember these words, and many a time regretted that he had not taken his friend's advice; for it proved true, as he had said – the Pizarros did not forget!

He found Alvarado's force drawn up on the opposite bank of the river Abançay, which was crossed by a bridge and also had a fording-place, though the general current was deep. He posted his soldiers at the bridge, but detached a body of them, after thus attracting Alvarado's attention, and availing himself of the ford, fell upon his rear with such effect that the battle was over soon after it began. Alvarado was made prisoner, and, save for a few soldiers who escaped and fled back to Lima, all were captured who did not voluntarily desert and join the victorious force under Almagro.

That was the time, probably, when he marched triumphantly back to Cuzco, that Almagro's fortunes touched "high-watermark." By the accessions from Alvarado's army, his force had nearly doubled, and one can hardly wonder at his self-importance, when, soon after his return to the capital, he was vainly importuned by an embassage from Pizarro to abate his pretensions and await a decision from the crown. This body of dignitaries was headed by one Espinosa, who had been a silent partner with Almagro, Luque, and Pizarro at the outset in Panama, and is said to have furnished the major portion of the funds upon which they depended for their first successes. But, though Almagro greatly honored him, he would not listen to his advice, which was to release his prisoners, retire from Cuzco, and await news from Spain.

"Nay! nay!" cried Almagro. "Though you may be my ancient friend, Licentiate, I cannot heed your advice. You know with what perfidy and contempt our partner, Francisco Pizarro, has rewarded us, retaining all the spoils for himself and bestowing upon those who aided him most the least portion of plunder.

"Say no more, no more, for I am resolved not only to retain control of this, my city of Cuzco – which now has been twice placed in my possession: once by Francisco's orders and once won by the sword – but also to march upon his new city of *Los Reyes* [Lima] and rout him out of it. For it is mine, falling as it does within my jurisdiction!"

"That will be seen when proved," answered Espinosa. "But I advise you, yes, adjure you, [18] not to come to close quarters with Francisco, for when aroused he is a lion."

"Ay, the king of *beasts*! that he is, I will admit; but I know him, and, knowing, fear him not. Say no more; we march tomorrow."

Taking Hernando Pizarro with him, but leaving Gonzalo and other important officers in Cuzco, Almagro set out for Lima, with the avowed intention of attacking his old partner in the city he had founded. He duly reached the valley of the Rimac, or Lima, indeed; but, though exasperated by the intelligence that Gonzalo Pizarro and Alvarado had escaped and had arrived ahead of him, he was eventually won over by Francisco's diplomacy to consent to an interview.

The two commanders met at Mala, a place on the high-road midway between Lima and Chincha, which latter Almagro had founded. All three places may still be found on the map, though they were in existence so early as the date of this interview, which was in mid-November, 1537. The erstwhile comrades met, with embraces and tears, and it could hardly have been surmised that one of them, at least, was even then plotting the destruction of the other.

There seemed, indeed, a prospect of their coming to terms, when, in the midst of it all, one of Almagro's attendants hastily entered the room and whispered in his ear, that Gonzalo Pizarro had moved a band of troopers up the road to intercept him. A horse was at the door, and, hastily mounting it, Almagro galloped off to his camp, leaving the baffled Pizarro in a rage.

The latter explained next day that his brother had moved without orders, and, Almagro affecting to believe it, negotiations were renewed, with the result that it was mutually agreed that Cuzco should remain in his hands for the time, and Hernando Pizarro should be released on condition that he sail for Spain within six weeks of that date. Further hostilities were to be suspended, each to hold what he had gained until the pleasure of the king was known.

The generous Almagro made all haste to acquaint Hernando with the fact that he was free, with his own hands releasing him from his fetters. In response to his expressed desire that they should henceforth be friends, Hernando replied, with a smile, "I trust we shall never be anything else than friends, Señor Mariscal," and warmly embraced him. He was then taken to Almagro's tent, where a banquet was spread in his honor, at which toasts were drunk to their future friendship and prosperity.

Nor was Francisco Pizarro behind his former partner in courtesy, for when Hernando was escorted to his camp, by a little band in which was included Almagro's son, afterwards his heir, he took particular pains to shower him with attentions, and sent him back to his father rejoicing. But, no sooner had the Almagro party left his presence, than Pizarro called a council of his officers and to them disclosed his perfidious designs. In brief, he purposed to break all the solemn pledges he had made to Almagro, and at once equip a force for the reduction of Cuzco, to march, if possible, before the marshal should regain that stronghold.

When Almagro heard the news he was astounded, his chivalrous nature hardly permitting him to entertain doubts of Pizarro's integrity; but Orgoñez reminded him of the remark he had made and the advice he had given. "You should have cut off Hernando's head," he said a second time, "for now he is going to march upon Cuzco, and, if he wins, will surely cut off yours."

These words were, alas! too true; for Hernando, notwithstanding his solemn oaths, upon his sacred honor, that he would ever regard Almagro as his friend, was prevailed upon by Francisco to take command of the force he was raising and pursue that "friend" to the death. By means of his spies, Almagro learned of this intention, and at once set out for the mountains. Hernando started a few days after, and thenceforth it was a race between the two as to which should first gain access to the city of Cuzco. Almagro won the race, though he was so infirm, from age and disease, that he had to be carried in a litter all the weary way. He won the race and gained the city, though he was so ill-advised that, on the approach of Hernando with his army, he marched out to meet him, instead of remaining behind his breastworks and compelling the attacking force to fight at a disadvantage.

Almagro made vigorous preparations for defence; but threw away all he had gained when he led his soldiers forth to the plain of Salinas, or the Salt-pits, where the final battle was fought. During days and nights the city had resounded with the ring of metal, as the hammers of the smiths clanged on plates of solid silver, which were to be transformed into breastplates for the infantry and horseshoes for the cavalry.

Clad in shining armor, horses shod with silver, the soldiers of Almagro marched out of the city and across the plain, taking up a position chosen by Orgoñez, who, for the first time in his long service under the marshal, committed an error of judgment. It was an error fatal to him, as well as to the fortunes of Almagro, for, descending from the mountains in battle array, the seven hundred soldiers of Pizarro savagely attacked the five hundred of Almagro, and, hemming them in between a sierra and a swamp, where they could not use their cavalry (the marshal's strongest reliance), they poured into their ranks such a fire of musketry that the "Almagrists" finally broke and fled.

The "Pizarrists" were armed with an improved arquebuse, which carried a tremendous charge of powder and a twin shot united by a chain. Gallant Orgoñez raged up and down the field, vainly seeking an encounter with Hernando Pizarro. Mistaking another cavalier for the commander, he ran him through with his sword and another with his lance, but in the midst of his career was struck by a chain-shot, which brought him senseless to the ground. Before he could revive he was disarmed and stabbed to the heart by a common soldier, and thus perished Almagro's leader and chief general.

Meanwhile, Hernando himself was seeking for Orgoñez, having donned a bright-colored surcoat over his corselet and stuck a long plume in his helmet, to make himself conspicuous. For he was a brave man, even if a cruel and treacherous one, and shunned no encounter with the enemy. In his search he ran across a renegade from Alvarado's army, one Pedro de Lerma, who had told Almagro how to make the feint by which he won before. Both men were caballeros, or horsemen of distinction, and they charged at each other as though in a tourney, coming together with a crash heard far over the field. Both were dismounted by the shock, but Lerma received a wound which disabled him, while Hernando still fought on to victory.

While these individual encounters were taking place, the cavalry of both sides were not behind their commanders in valor. They charged full upon one another, horse and rider going down in the tremendous onslaught, at which the surrounding hills re sounded with yells and howls, as though a band of demons had been watching and waiting for that hour and deed. For thousands of Indians had gathered on the heights, whence they looked down upon the fighting Spaniards, gloating over the bloody scene, and rejoicing that, at last, whichever side won, they were in some measure receiving their revenge. After the battle was over, they descended to the plain and roamed about like ghouls, avenging themselves for the plundering of their homes and temples by stripping the slain of weapons, armor, and even of garments, leaving the naked corpses stark upon the field of death.

And Almagro. What had become of him? He was so stricken by disease that he could not mount his horse, but lay in a litter watching the fight from a near hill. He saw the opponents come together, severally shouting: "The king and Pizarro!" "The king and Almagro!"

He heard the crash of musketry, the shock of charging cavalry, and finally the shouts of the victors. Realizing that all was lost, that fate had turned against him, he fled towards the city and shut himself up in the fortress, which he should not have abandoned in the first place. There he was found, thence he was taken to Hernando Pizarro, by whom he was ordered placed in the same dungeon he himself had occupied with his brother, Gonzalo.

The conqueror received him graciously, even inquiring as to his health, for which he seemed very solicitous. Almagro was flattered by this attention and his fears were soothed by these inquiries; but far different would have been his feelings had he known the reason for Hernando's solicitude. He had been heard to say, when it was reported that Almagro was "like to die of his disease," "Heaven forbid that it come to pass before he falls into my hands!" He looked upon him, indeed, in the light in which the cannibal views a victim he is fattening for the sacrifice. Not a day passed that Hernando did not send Almagro some delicacy from his table, and therefore the old marshal soon recovered his strength and cheerful spirits. But, though he was promised that his release should come when the governor arrived, somehow that worthy was long in arriving. One day, when he had recovered sufficiently to walk about and receive visits from his friends, he was suddenly seized by some soldiers and dragged to the great square, where, after the pretence of a trial, he was sentenced to death.

Then he realized, bewildered as he was, the extent of Hernando Pizarro's perfidy, and when he next appeared, in response to his pleadings, he reproached him with ingratitude. He reminded him that he had never shed the blood of a Pizarro, though he had held two of the family in his power. And was his clemency thus to be rewarded?

Hernando shrugged his shoulders and coldly replied: "What you did not do to me when you had me in your power, I now do to you, having you in my power. You should not have been so remiss. But I wonder that one who has faced death so many times should now be afraid of it!"

"It is not so much the death I fear, as the disgrace," replied Almagro, humbly. "But, since our Lord and Saviour also feared it, though he endured it, what more can be expected of me, a mere man and a sinner?"

That night, as he slept, two persons stealthily entered Almagro's dungeon. One was a priest, the other – the executioner! That night, two hours later, a limp and lifeless body was borne into the great square, where it was beheaded and then left exposed till morning.

It was Almagro. He had been strangled. "A Pizarro never forgets!"

XIX

HOW PIZARRO WAS ASSASSINATED

1541

ALL the Pizarros put on mourning for Almagro, and two of them, Hernando and Gonzalo, followed his remains to the tomb. The third member of this precious trio, Governor Francisco, was on his way from Lima while the trial was being conducted, and is said to have purposely delayed his arrival at Cuzco in order to leave Hernando a free hand. He desired the death of his partner and rival, but did not wish it to appear that he was privy to it. Hernando, it seems, had no such scruples, and when, after sending a message to the governor (who was then at Xauxa), asking what he should do with Almagro, he received in reply: "Deal with him so that he shall cause us no more trouble," he followed these instructions literally.

Almagro had, indeed, been put where he would cause them no more trouble; but he had left an heir to his claims, as well as friends who revered his memory and would avenge his death. He left a son, the offspring of an Indian woman of Panama, and like himself illegitimate, but to whom he was tenderly attached. Young Diego Almagro had followed his father to the field and been with him constantly since he could stand alone. Just before the marshal was executed, he was sent to meet the governor, who received him graciously and promised him protection, at the same time assuring him his father should not be killed. Even at that moment, however, Almagro the elder was being strangled in his cell, and the boy was thus left at the mercy of his enemies.

When Francisco Pizarro received tidings of Almagro's death he was at the bridge of Abançay, where his rival had fought and defeated Alvarado. He was greatly affected, even to tears, and his frame trembled with emotion, though his grief was not so poignant but that he could hide it successfully on his entrance into Cuzco a few days later. With blare of trumpet and beat of drum, banners flying and horses prancing, Governor Pizarro entered a second time the city of the sun, to receive the homage of its inhabitants. He was richly dressed, wearing a splendid suit of velvet adorned with gems, which had been sent him from Mexico by Hernando Cortés.

Establishing himself in the palace, he administered the government, while his brother, Hernando, made preparations for a voyage to Spain. It was a desperate move for Hernando, who, in doubt as to the reception he would receive, gathered a vast quantity of treasure as a gift to propitiate the emperor, perchance he should be incensed at his treatment of Almagro.

His fears were well founded, as it proved, for soon after arriving in Spain he was summoned to trial, and eventually cast into prison, from which he did not emerge for twenty-three years! When finally released, he found not one friend alive to welcome him, it is said, save his niece, Francisco's child by the daughter of Inca Atahuallpa, whom the governor lived with after he had murdered her father. This niece, in whose blood ran the blood of Pizarro and the Incas, took pity on Hernando and married him. Whether they lived happily together is not known; but they lived long, and Hernando attained the great age of one hundred years, surviving, it is believed, every comrade of his who had taken part in the conquest of Peru.

All his brothers had died by the hand of violence long before his term of imprisonment expired, and the first to fall a victim to the hatred and lust for vengeance he himself had engendered was Francisco, the governor, the marquis, the despot, and the "tyrant of Peru."

Before he set sail for Spain, Hernando had said to his brother, the marquis: "Beware the men of Chile! Disperse them over the country, and do not allow them to gather into bands of any size, for they are desperate and vengeful. They are already plotting, and mean to have revenge for what you and I have done to them."

"Ha, ha," laughed Francisco; "I shall take care of Almagro's men. I will make paupers of them all; there shall not be a single cloak between any dozen of them. But, strike me? No, they dare not."

"But they will dare," answered Hernando. "Would that I could be here to protect thee, brother mine."

With these words, and after many embraces, the brothers who had been chiefly instrumental in the conquest parted, and never saw each other again. The one went home to serve a score of years in prison; the other remained, to dig with his own hands the grave into which he was sent by the assassin's dagger.

Had Pizarro desired to hasten his own ending, he could not have taken surer means to do so than he did. While as brave as a lion, he was impolitic and indiscreet. He dispersed Almagro's followers, and deprived them of everything they owned, at the same time rewarding his adherents with farms, mines, flocks of llamas, and droves of Indians. His brothers, especially, were recompensed beyond any ten or twenty other cavaliers, who had fought in scores of battles, so that there was great murmuring on every side. In order to quiet those murmurings, the governor sent off Gonzalo, with a large body of troops, to seek out and if possible destroy the Inca Manco, who had descended from his mountain fastnesses and was waging a guerilla warfare against the scattered settlements. Swooping down from his strongholds, with bands of fleet-footed warriors, the Inca carried desolation into many a district, and committed great depredations. Gonzalo took his trail, but was unable to subdue him, though the two had many encounters, in which, if he did not win the victory, the Inca so far crippled his adversary that he could not pursue him to his secret haunts in the mountains.

At last Pizarro tried to propitiate the Inca with gifts, and sent presents by an African slave; but his emissary was murdered on the way. In revenge, the cruel Pizarros ordered one of the favorite wives of the Inca, who had fallen into their hands, to be scourged to death while naked and bound to a tree. She endured the torture with such fortitude that the rude soldiers were amazed; but no sentiment of pity stirred their hearts, it seemed, for they made no protest to the governor. Except for his cruelty to the Indians and his shameful treatment of Almagro's men, Pizarro 's conduct was now most commendable. He devoted himself altogether to the development of Peru's vast resources, to the increasing of her commerce, and the founding of cities. In a few years from his initial attempts at city-making, he had established on a secure basis such places as Lima, Callao, Truxillo, and Arequipa. He delighted in promoting their growth and adorning them with splendid [19] structures; nor was he interested in them to the exclusion of his concern for the country at large. He imported great quantities of seeds and plants from Europe, also cattle, sheep, and swine, which flourished amazingly in the land he had adopted as his own.

But it was in Lima, the new "City of the Kings," that he expended most. There he built a splendid palace; there he settled the pick of his soldiers; there he resolved to live out the remainder of his days. Surrounding himself with a large retinue of dependents, and in every way evincing that he belonged to the class known as hidalgos (though he had hewn his way solely by his sword), he maintained in Lima the state of a great grandee. Yet he was always simple in dress and manners, preferring comfort to display, and while avaricious in the pursuit of gold, was lavish in the spending of it.

He had chosen as companion a daughter of the Inca Atahuallpa (as already stated), and with her and their growing family of children lived in great content, surrounded with every luxury. In this manner, with all his wishes gratified, and as independent of control as the emperor himself, Pizarro lived at ease in Lima. Though he could not read or write, and though he had found it impossible to supply these deficiencies of his early education late in life, he was possessed of a sturdy good sense, which enabled him to govern his vast realm and diverse peoples wisely.

No portion of Peru was so distant, so wild and rugged, that he did not keep it within his ken and inform himself constantly of what was occurring there . He sent out expeditions to explore and conquer: as, Valdivia to Chile and his brother, Gonzalo, to Quito and the Land of Cinnamon. The gallant and dashing Gonzalo, youngest of his brothers, and his favorite, he despatched to Quito as governor, with instructions to penetrate, if possible, to the mysterious country beyond the Cordilleras. Taking with him three hundred and fifty soldiers, horse and foot, and four thousand

Indians, Gonzalo set out on his perilous journey. He was young, ambitious, enthusiastic, and loyal. Two years he was absent on this expedition, and when he returned the whole aspect of political affairs had changed, his brother was dead, and the government overthrown.

Soon after establishing himself in Quito, Gonzalo had led his little army over the mountains, setting out in January, 1540. After passing the regions of fire and snow, he plunged into the tropical forests which opened and swallowed him up. For nearly two years he wandered in those vast forests, where the towering trees almost hid the sun, and where boa-constrictors, jaguars, and alligators were the only visible inhabitants, save for the birds infrequently seen.

The sufferings of Gonzalo and his companions were intense. Their clothing was torn off by the branches of trees or rotted from the damp; their provisions became exhausted and they were forced to eat their horses, then their dogs, a thousand of which latter animals they had taken along for hunting down the natives. They were extremely ferocious, and could not have been put to a better use than that in which they served the starving Spaniards. When horses and dogs were gone, the only food available consisted of roots and herbs, upon which the miserable explorers lived for months.

They found the forests of cinnamon, but could not make use of the aromatic bark; they saw signs of gold, but could not carry it away; and when in the midst of their greatest perils, they made a discovery which has linked the name of Pizarro with the greatest river in the world. Deeming it impossible to return to Peru, Gonzalo caused a boat to be built, from green timbers cut in the forest, put together with nails made from horseshoes, and calked with rags from the soldiers' raiment. It was not large enough to contain them all, but fifty of the feebler men embarked in it, commanded by Francisco de Orellana, who had come from Gonzalo's own town of Truxillo. They embarked, and the swift current swept them away, never more to be seen by Gonzalo; but they emerged at last on the Atlantic, and carried to Spain tidings of the great river Amazon.

With the disappearance of the rude brigantine, the soldiers yielded themselves to despair; but Gonzalo was equal to the emergency, and, though they had then been a year in the forest, and another year elapsed before they emerged, he eventually led them through all besetting perils – all that was left of them, eighty soldiers and two thousand Indians – over the mountains, and out upon the plains of Quito. They were welcomed by their friends as if they had risen from their graves; and, indeed, for two years they had been as effectually cut off from the world as if buried beneath the ground. No word had reached them of what had happened in Peru, but when they heard they were thunderstruck, their gallant leader especially being overcome with grief.

Gonzalo had left his brother, the governor, in the midst of his family, with every prospect of passing the remainder of his days in serene content. But the elder Pizarro had committed the fatal mistake of trusting men whose memories of the past were filled with bitterness. He himself never forgot an insult nor forgave one. Why, then, should he assume that other men had shorter memories?

He allowed the son of Almagro not only to live in Lima, after he had deprived him of his father's legacies, but to occupy a house on the same square with himself. He heard, from time to time, rumors of gatherings in that house which boded no good to himself: of meetings at night, attended by dark-browed conspirators against his power, perhaps against his life. He knew that the "men of Chile" had latterly come in from the country, where they had lived for years in poverty. By twos and threes they had stealthily gained admittance to the city, and, growing bold at Pizarro's indifference, were wont to assemble in Almagro's house. The governor's secretary, one Picado, warned him that these men were plotting against his life; but Pizarro was too brave, too self-confident, to take alarm.

"Let them plot, and much good may it do them," he answered, carelessly. "The poor devils have suffered enough, in sooth; let us leave them to their misery."

A few days later he came to Pizarro in genuine alarm. "Your excellency, " he stammered, "I have a story you must hear and must heed. It comes from Father –, who obtained it in confession from a man of Chile. It is this: Only last night they met – twenty of them – at Almagro's house. Juan de Rada sat at the head of the table. Yes, he is the leader of the conspirators. Ha, you start! for only yesterday he was walking with you in your garden. You taxed him with buying a suit of mail and a sword, and what did he say, your excellency?"

"He said," responded Pizarro, lightly, "that he had heard I was buying lances to slay the men of Chile with, and so would be prepared. And I replied, 'Please God, Juan de Rada, I shall do no such thing,' and gave him some oranges, at which he kissed my hand, departing well pleased."

"Ha, yes! Well pleased that he had fooled your excellency! But, know you, he it is who has sworn to waylay you to-morrow, coming from morning mass, and stab you to the heart! It is true, oh, believe me. Be warned in time, and send those men of Chile all to prison."

"I might do worse, in sooth. But who told you? Father –? Ho! I have it. It is a trick of his. He is tired of being a priest, and wants me to make him bishop!" And Pizarro, laughing loudly at his jest, turned away and left Picado speechless.

But he was not so insensible to the warning as he had made the secretary believe, for he sought out his chief judge, Velasquez, told him the story, and asked his advice. The judge listened intently, then replied: "I will inquire into this affair, your excellency. But, meanwhile, have no fear," he added, pompously; "for no harm shall come to you while I hold the rod of justice in my hands!"

The "rod of justice" was no mere figure of speech, but a wand, which the judge was wont by custom to carry. It fell out that his words came true, for no harm came to Pizarro while he held it in his hands, as will soon be shown.

Sunday came, June 26, 1541; but Pizarro did not go to church that day, giving out that he was ill. The conspirators were baffled – for there were conspirators, and they had sworn to kill Pizarro, as stated. They watched through the latticed windows of Almagro's house all the morning for the portly figure of the governor and his brilliant retinue, but in vain. At last it dawned upon them that Pizarro had been warned.

"Betrayed!" they muttered, looking at one another furtively and fumbling their swords. "Then there is nothing but flight!" exclaimed one; but Rada turned upon him instantly with: "Flight! Not for me. No, nor for any one of us. The first one shall be run through with my sword!"

He threw open the door and darted out of the house, closely followed by the rest, with drawn swords held aloft, and shouting: "Long live the king! Death to the tyrant!"

"Who is the tyrant?" asked an on-looker, coolly, of another.

"Oh, the marquis, I suppose. They are going to kill him."

His death had been imminent so long, his enemies so many, that, the hour now arrived, no surprise was manifested. And the hour was noon, when the streets of the city were mostly deserted. Some cavaliers, however, who perhaps had been notified to be in readiness, joined the conspirators as they hurried across the plaza, and swelled the shout of "Down with the tyrant! Long live the king!"

Pizarro was at dinner, together with a few friends enjoying his mid-day repast. Though he had been warned, he felt secure in his palace, with its strong gates, its massive walls, and the few faithful servitors on duty. But this sense of false security was his undoing, for the conspirators easily entered the courtyard, the gate of which was open, cut down a domestic who ventured to oppose them, and dashed up the broad stairway to the dining-hall. Ahead of them, fleeing in terror, darted a servant, who woke the echoes with his cries of "Help! help! The men of Chile are here to murder the marquis!"

Pizarro heard the cries, and could not but be aware what they signified. But he coolly said to a friend, who stood by, one Francisco de Chaves. "Close the door, Chaves, and bar it. Only give me time to get my armor on."

He and his half-brother, Martin Alcantara, darted for their armor, and were struggling to get into it all the while that band of conspirators raged at the door. If Chaves had obeyed Pizarro's command, there might be a different story to tell; but instead of closing the door instantly, he held it ajar, either from curiosity or in order to parley with the assassins, and that moment's delay was fatal. One of them reached in and drove a sword through his heart, and then, tumbling the bleeding

body down the stairs, they all rushed up, with loud cries of "Where is the marquis? Show us the tyrant!"

The fifteen or twenty retainers in the room thrust themselves before the throng, and in the mêlée several were slain, as well as two of the conspirators. Martin Alcantara hastened to their assistance, and was quickly cut down. At sight of his brother on the floor, bathed in blood, Pizarro could contain himself no longer. Casting aside the corselet he was trying to fasten on, he wrapped his cloak around one arm, and brandishing his sword, dashed himself against the group of men, whom he met at the entrance to the antechamber. He cut and slashed so vigorously that they all fell back, while he cried: "Ho, come on! Come on! You think to kill me in my own house! We shall see!"

While he was holding them at bay, his guests cast themselves from the windows into the garden, and among them was the boastful judge, Velasquez. He had his rod of office with him, and in the exigency of the moment, in order to be able to use both his hands, took it in his mouth. Thus it came literally true that Pizarro was not harmed while the judge had his rod in his hands, as was afterwards jestingly said.

Meanwhile, the conspirators were not idle. By relieving one another in turn, they began to weary Pizarro, who still fought on, however, though against fearful odds. At last the chief conspirator, Rada, who was behind the rest as they struggled in the narrow doorway, shouted hoarsely: "Why are ye so long about it? Kill him, and have done! So saying, he threw the man in front upon Pizarro, who instantly ran him through with his sword. Before he could withdraw it, the fierce Rada was upon him with a dagger, and several swords were plunged into his body. Mortally stricken, he fell reeling to the floor, with the cry of "Jesu" – Saviour – on his lips.

The blood from his many ghastly wounds formed a pool on the floor, in which, with his forefinger, he traced the sign of the cross. As he bent over to kiss the holy symbol, another swift stroke descended, and the Conqueror of Peru was no more.

78229811R00049

Made in the USA
San Bernardino, CA
03 June 2018